Reinforce Your Gym

The Firepower You Need To Build A Million Dollar Fitness Business

BY

Dustin Bogle

Copyright © 2023 by Dustin Bogle.

All rights reserved. No part of this publication may be reproduced, distributed, or transmitted in any form or by any means, including photocopying, recording, or other electronic or mechanical methods, without the prior written permission of the author, except in the case of brief quotations embodied in critical reviews and certain other non-commercial uses permitted by copyright law.

Ordering Information: Quantity sales. Special discounts are available on quantity purchases by corporations, associations, and others. Orders by U.S. trade bookstores and wholesalers.

www.DreamStartersPublishing.com

Table of Contents

Dedication..4

Introduction...6

I Just Need More Leads....................................... 19

The 3 Cs of Coaching... 25

Your Ideal Customer 32

Demographics 32

Psychographics... 32

Offers So Good They Sell Themselves 42

How To Get Infinite Leads.................................. 53

The Convicted Lawyer.. 69

The Fortune Follow Up System 76

The C.H.A.R.M Sales Process 91

Creating The Next Hill 101

97% Retention All Year Long..............................109

Lead The Way 122

If They're Not Gold, We Hold............................136

Tools for High Performing Teams........................150

The Root of All Team Problems 159

Is This Your Best Work?.....................................173

Gym Owner Success Stories...............................179

Dedication

To my darling wife MaryBeth, and my beautiful children, Logan and Chloe.

This book is dedicated to our family. You are "the why" behind my work ethic. I can't let you down. I won't let you down.

MaryBeth, you are the love of my life, my best friend, my partner in crime and my constant companion. Your love and support have been my anchor through the highs and lows of life. You have always believed in me, even when I doubted myself, and your faith in my has given me strength to preserve. Thank you for being the best wife in the world.

Logan and Chloe, you are the light of my life, my pride and joy, my miracles. I am blessed to be your father. You are the reason I wake up every day with a smile on my face. Your pure hearts, boundless energy and infectious laughter have brought so much joy to my life. I cherish every moment I've spent with you. You teach me as much as I teach you.

I dedicate this book to you as a symbol of my gratitude and love. May it serve as a reminder that we live in the greatest country in the world that allows us the freedom to pursue The American Dream. The magic of our dreams can come true if we are willing to put in the work. I hope it inspires you to chase your passion and believe in yourself.

Introduction

The doors busted open and hundreds of angry wrestling fans were running toward me. I thought I was going to die right there in Mexico City. I saw the anger in their eyes. They had every right to be mad. Their hard earned money was being taken and no refunds were offered. They wanted to hurt us as payback.

Let me backup a minute. Before I was a Gym Owner, I was a Pro Wrestler for 10 years. I got to wrestle around the world against local indy wrestlers and famous 80s superstars like Marty Jannetty, Tito Santana and Haku. And I've even wrestled some of the superstars you see on TV today - Sami Zayn, Seth Rollins, Cesaro and more!

My childhood friends, The Young Bucks, and I ran our own wrestling company called High Risk Wrestling. Today, they are Executive Vice Presidents of All Elite Wrestling, a popular wrestling show that airs on TNT weekly. My brother, Brandon Cutler, is their manager.

At the beginning of my career, I wrestled under the name Diablo. I had long hair, flame designs on my gear and angry metal music as I walked to the ring with a robe that had devil horns. Like most young adults, I needed to express my rebellious energy. My outlet was pro wrestling.

It was punk rock. Not your traditional career path. And just plain fun even though you get paid $20 per match. Most of the time you wrestle for free in your early years. Just go on YouTube and search Diablo High Risk Wrestling" or Cutler Brothers" to see footage of me in action.

For those wondering, yes wrestling is a pre-planned show. I think the cat is out of the bag by now. But the best wrestlers, like magicians, can suspend your belief. They can get you emotionally involved in the match by using facial expressions, body language and storytelling.

In wrestling, you either get booked by the promoter as a babyface (good guy) or a heel (bad guy). I always enjoyed being the heel. There's nothing like knocking a soda out of someone's hand or ripping their sign in half. It's all part of the show.

Ok back to Mexico with the angry crowd that wanted to kill me. I was asked to go to Mexico for a two week tour. The promoter saw me perform at a lucha libre show in LA and was impressed. He wanted me to be in the main event as the heel against a lucha legend Rey Mysterio Sr. - the uncle of WWE Superstar Rey Mysterio Jr.

I didn t need much convincing. I was in.

Lucha Libre in Mexico is the second most popular sport in the country, right behind soccer. The fans can get intense. I had batteries thrown at my head. Cups of yellow liquid that I thought was beer. It wasn t.

We were four days into the two week tour but the fight night was different. We were in Mexico City and something was off with the wrestlers. I could sense it somehow. The luchas weren t smiling and joking around as much. There was tension but not knowing the language I couldn t figure out what was going on.

Finally, I noticed that Rey Mysterio Sr. was not getting dressed into his ring gear and the show already started. We were going to be up next very soon. I decided to ask him what was going on.

Rey Mysterio Sr. explained My friend. Our match isn t happening tonight." He could tell I was confused when I made a face. The promoter has no money. The luchas are walking out on him. Please follow me. The fans will be very unhappy."

Later on I found out the promoter wasn t very good at his job. He had top tier talent on the card. These stadiums should have been packed but they weren t because he skipped on advertising. One of my first lessons in marketing. As a result, he didn t sell enough tickets which means he didn t have enough money to pay the wrestlers.

Mysterio Sr. motioned to grab my suitcase. We quickly exited through the back door as I heard the ring announcer begin to explain to the fans the situation. They got two matches but were promised twelve.

The wrestlers who draw the crowd" are the most popular wrestlers that get the most fans to buy tickets. They put butts in seats. These fans were getting jibbed from seeing the main draw - Rey Mysterio Sr. They were not going to be happy.

We sprinted to our tour bus and got onboard. As I walked up the steps, I looked out the giant tinted windows and I saw the stadium doors burst open. A horde of angry fans came out and pointed at the tour bus. My eyes got big and my heart rate went up.

Let s get the hell out of here." I yelled at the bus driver who didn t speak a word of English. But he could tell in the urgency of my voice that we needed to move fast.

The wrestling fans surrounded the bus and started shaking it. They demanded we come out and perform the rest of the show. We were all big strong guys who could defend ourselves but there were only 30 of us and hundreds of them.

The bus driver fired up the engine and we started moving slowly. The mob moved alongside the bus banging on the glass. I thought to myself This is it. I m going to die." I had a cheap flip phone that didn t work internationally so I couldn t call for help.

The bus started picking up speed but the crowd was not going to let us get away. They started running alongside the bus and throwing rocks at the windows. The bus began to go faster and eventually outran the angry mob.

A few minutes later we drove into a small town. The bus driver thought of a clever idea and backed the bus into a nearby alleyway.

It was midnight at this point. We took off our wrestling gear and put on our street clothes to blend in. We didn't know if the fans would try to follow us all the way to the town. So we spread out in a few groups and got some street tacos.

Wrestling is known for wild moments but this one had us all shaken up.

I had no idea where I was, my phone died and I had no money. I was completely dependent on the payday from this tour to get home. I didn't bring any cash with me and had no credit card. Smart thinking right?

Luckily, one of the refs was a former employee of the WWE. He showed me photos of himself holding the Undertaker s arms up in victory after winning a match in the 80 s. He could tell I was vulnerable and needed help.

He offered to drive me to the airport in the morning and pay for my flight home. I was overjoyed and told him I would send money back the minute I got home. He assured me that it wasn t necessary. I have no idea how I would have gotten home without his generosity. That's the brotherhood of wrestling. Always having each other's backs.

On the flight home to SoCal, I reflected on the crazy tour but one topic kept popping up in my mind - money. I was a struggling personal trainer on the weekdays and struggling pro wrestler on the weekends. I wanted the struggle to end.

I looked back and saw a common thread…

- Why was the crowd so upset? Money.

- What caused me to be stranded in Mexico? Money.
- Why did the promoter go to jail? Money.

It was at that moment I made a decision to figure out my money problems once and for all. I didn t like the idea that my income was dependent upon someone else. That s where I started to connect with my entrepreneurial energy.

In sports you can get a huge opportunity based on your ability to score points or assist. Pro wrestling is sports entertainment. It's a show and opportunities come to you based on approval by the fans and promoter.

You need to win the popularity game to get ahead in wrestling. And I just wasn t built for all the politics involved. I wanted to control my own future. I wanted to take control of my financial situation.

Money can be emotionally charging.

It can get you excited and motivated to work hard but it can also cause stress, fear and anger. People can get violent over it. Couples argue about it. Friendships and families are destroyed because of it. It s one of the main causes of stress in a person s life.

But at the same time, it can be the source of so much positivity. Money can create jobs, drive innovation, fuel charities and create freedom. It can give you options that you wouldn't have without it.

The wrestling promoter was a poor steward of money. He gives business owners a bad name. But just because you have had experiences with people who misuse money doesn t mean it s a bad thing. We give money meaning based on our experiences.

Money is like a gun. The danger or safety comes from the person using it.

I was determined to find a way to make money flow to me. And I would do it in a way that is about helping others.

I didn t want to focus on being the champion.
I wanted to make others the champion.

I wanted to find something that made me feel good while providing endless opportunities for myself and those around me. I wanted to take everyone along for the ride.

That s when I went all in on the fitness industry.

And within four years I built a 7-figure fitness business. I didn t do it alone. I hired mentors. Ran countless tests. Coached thousands of sessions. Sold millions in fitness programs. I know the ins-and-outs of running a gym because I ve done every job that exists.

After being a Gym Owner for over a decade and running 6 locations, I can tell you that I m not smarter or better than you. In fact, I ve failed many times but I look at them as learning lessons. Each one got me closer and closer to a winning strategy.

This book is a collection of my winning strategies so you can build the business of your dreams.

Why am I so passionate about helping Gym Owners?
Why don t I focus on my own gyms and mind my own business?

To be honest, I m disturbed when I read about the obesity statistics in the US. I know I can t make a big enough dent alone. We need our entire industry to join forces against our common enemy.

As of 2023, the CDC says that 42.4% of Americans are obese. They predict that 50% of Americans will be obese and 20% of the global population will be obese by 2030.

We are at war with obesity!

It s killing our families. People are dying too early of lifestyle related diseases. These are 100% preventable deaths. It s happening in my family and it s probably affecting your family too.

Here s how I see things…

- Gyms are the forward operating base
- Coaches are the troops on the front lines

- Sessions are the battlefield where we fight to strengthen our mind and body
- Gym Owners are the generals opening safe zones for people to take back their health

And I want to help you reinforce your gym and add firepower to your impact and income.

Reinforce: to make strong, to strengthen by additional assistance, material, or support.
Firepower: the capacity to deliver effective fire on a target

I m on a mission to move our obesity numbers in the opposite direction. We must be relentless until we see the obesity percentages drop. There s billions of people who need our help.

Right now they are being given pills, surgeries and quick fixes that are a band-aid fix.

We need to educate and lead the public to the path of long term success. That s the mission of our industry and I know you want to have a big impact. The quality of life that comes from having a healthy body is priceless.

People with pain in their body, excess body fat, negative self-talk, and an unhealthy relationship with food need your help. Being healthy is the ultimate gift to give yourself and others. It s not an easy fight but it s worth it.

Now let s get to work on building you a wildly profitable business so you can make the world a healthier place.

SECTION I

BUILD YOUR LEAD MACHINE

Chapter 1

I Just Need More Leads

Let s kick things off by clearly defining a lead. The way I refer to leads in this book is anyone who has given you contact information (name, phone, email) and not currently a client.

A lead is someone you desires more info about your program and you want to sell into your service.

They could come from Facebook Ads, walk-ins, referrals, website, social media messages or any path that leads to your business.

If you have 1,200 contacts in your CRM or database and 200 of them are members then you have 1,000 leads. Make sense?

I used to believe that more leads would solve all my problems.

Most gym don't need more leads, they need more leadership.

I will touch on that later in Section III. For now, lets focus on marketing.

After running multiple gyms for over a decade I can tell you from experience that it s not a cure-all. It s a two edged sword.

On one hand, getting steady leads allows you to get reps. You get to more at-bat's which helps to sharpen your skills and get better at follow up and sales.

On the other hand, if you have strong lead flow and they are going through a crappy client experience then you are burning your leads.

Getting too many leads when you are not ready for them can burn your goodwill with the marketplace. Now you can get reverse word-of-mouth, which is when customers actively tell others to not use your service.

A negative client experience is when someone reaches out to a gym but doesn't get contacted for days. Maybe the sales process is too pushy and they don't feel like the sales rep cares about them.

The early stages of the client experience is when they have the most questions and have the most doubt and fear. Even after buying, they are still unsure and could experience buyers remorse.

Have you ever had someone signup for your program and then stop coming in after 1-2 workouts? Some Gym Owners would label these people as quitters and not fully committed.

But maybe they don t know what normal soreness is from a first workout. They might think they did something wrong and injured themselves. They don't know it's first time soreness".

Your service has two main aspects...

- Product - what they get (workouts, coaching, etc.)
- Experience - how they feel interacting with the company

Most Gym Owners focus too much on product and not enough on customer experience. As a result, they are churning and burning through potential amazing customers.

To really build a lead machine, you must have a strong product and client experience. That way you are ready for the surge that will be coming soon.

Trust me, we are going to get to lead generating strategies but we want to make sure the product and experience is dialed-in first. That way these people stay with you for years!

This is a mental adjustment. Instead of thinking "I need more leads", it's a shift to "how can I get more leads to buy and stay."

Most gyms don't need more leads. They need to improve their product and client experience.

Here's a breakdown of what it would look like if you just added 8 net clients per month for 12 months.

Month 1 >> 150 Members + 8 Net
Month 2 >> 158 Members + 8 Net
Month 3 >> 166 Members + 8 Net
Month 4 >> 174 Members + 8 Net
Month 5 >> 182 Members + 8 Net
Month 6 >> 190 Members + 8 Net
Month 7 >> 198 Members + 8 Net
Month 8 >> 206 Members + 8 Net
Month 9 >> 214 Members + 8 Net
Month 10 >> 222 Members + 8 Net
Month 11 >> 230 Members + 8 Net
Month 12 >> 238 Members + 8 Net

Final Results
Month 1 = 150 Members
Month 12 = 246 Members

That's almost 100 NET MEMBERS!!

That would require you to add 2 net clients per week, 8 per month and maintain an average of 97% retention.

We will get you there but it will take hard work - which I know you're not afraid of. Much like coaching a fat-loss client on long term results, we are going to attack the problems in sequence. It's a classic staircase format. One step builds off the last.

Improving your business in the order will yield the best results.

Give yourself brutally honest feedback.

If you believe you are strong lead generation, then you can move on to the next area of focus - lead nurture. If you feel like lead generation could improve, then keep reading the upcoming chapters. Lets start building your lead machine!

Value Bomb 💣

Rate Your Customer Experience and Lead Flow

- Look at Your Week #1 Customer Experience....
  - Rate Your Client Onboarding On a Scale of 1-10
  - How Can You Reduce Friction For The Client?
    (Fewer Steps, Common Confusion, Recurring Issues)
  - Do You Have Weekly Reports to Check Client Attendance?
  - Do You Have a First Workout Attendance Check-In?

- How Often Do You Check-In with Clients In The First 90 Days?

- Look at Your Lead Generation
  - Rate Your Lead Generation On a Scale of 1-10
  - How Many Leads Do You Average Monthly? (Don t Guess, Pull The 90 Day Report)

Chapter 2

The 3 Cs of Coaching

Value is one of those words that s elusive. People throw it around but most people don't stop and define what it means. What might be valuable to one person, might not be valuable to the next. That s why it s so important to define so you can deliver value to individuals who want what you offer.

Before we dive into the business strategies to grow a gym, we have to start with the actual service you provide. The entire business is built on this so it s important to dial it in before you sell it to the marketplace.

The better your service, the more word of mouth you will get. Let s make sure they are saying good things. That all begins with the value you deliver in your daily sessions.

You are a service based business but there s far more to it than meets the eye.

I ve coached tens of thousands of sessions so everything I share is from real world experience. I've had thousands of conversations with clients about the service we provide. And with over two decades of experience, I can share with with you the pattern that I spotted.

Three words kept coming when I asked clients over the years what they value most from their Coach.

I packaged them into something I call the 3 C s of Coaching.

Correct

This is the first C because it s the most popular. Most clients hire a Trainer or Coach because they want someone to show them how to fix their form. They want corrections so they can stay safe and see the best results from their training. Coaches refer to them as coaching cues" which are short, easy-to-understand phrases that help a client to fix their form.

For example, when a client is doing a TRX row exercise, you can tell them to imagine an orange between their shoulder blades. And when they perform a rep, they should squeeze their back so they can squeeze the orange and create orange juice.

Another coaching cue I like is called read the shirt" and I use it with squats. I tell the client that if they bend over and point their chest toward the ground then I can t read their shirt. I inform them that I should be able to read the writing on their shirt during the entire squat movement.

Another component of correction is to break beliefs and educate. We know that the fitness industry is plagued by myths and misinformation.

For example, how many clients have told you I m big boned" or my culture loves carbs" as a reason for them not losing weight. I take that as an opportunity to correct them.

I jokingly point out that there have been no human skeletons discovered with thicker bones than the rest and that's a silly myth. That gets the client to chuckle. Then I educate them on how we need to focus on things we can control (diet) and not waste energy focusing on what we can't.

When the carb loving culture" issue comes up, I let the client know that every culture in the world has a diet with carbs. So, your cultural diet isn t the cause for fat loss. It comes down to calories and we need to get you into a calorie deficit. Plain and simple.

Correcting a client can be done in a respectful and educational way. Our school system lacks nutrition and exercise education so it's up to us to destroy the myths and spread the truth.

Challenge

The second C is Challenge which means pushing your clients out of their comfort zone. It s easy to get stuck in a rut of doing the same exercises for the same reps with the same weight. Sometimes you need outside eyes to challenge you to lift more or change your tempo or increase your reps.

The challenge can be in their workouts, in the kitchen or a behavior. For example, if you know your clients need to eat more protein to hit their goals, organize a 30 day challenge.

You can ask them to commit to 3 workouts per week and they must hit their protein goal daily. You probably want that all year but when it's a short burst of intensity, it's more achievable for the client.

Great Coaches take mundane things and make them more fun.

Another example of challenging a client is when you push them outside their comfort zone. Maybe you have a client that hasn't been bringing the same excitement to their workouts. They probably need something exciting to chase. An active goal.

Challenge that client to take on something they perceive to be scary or impossible. It could be doing their first chin up or a full set of pushups.

Maybe the client always dreamed of completing a Spartan Run. Or they want to get fit by 40 and rock a bikini or dress at a party to show off their results.

These are all real world examples that I've helped my clients to achieve. And that person might have never achieved them without a Coach in their corner pushing them.

Cheer

Superheroes are known for their superpowers. Wolverine has rapid healing and Superman has superhuman strength. I firmly believe that the superpower of a Coach is encouragement. When you have someone cheering you on, you can do anything.

The word "encourage" means "to inspire courage."

There s a famous experiment where researchers had participants stand barefoot in a bucket of ice water. The participants stood in the bucket of ice water until it got so cold they couldn't stand it and had to get out of the bucket.

The researchers recorded everyone's best time. After that, they did a second round of the same experiment with the same participants but they changed a variable.

The researchers had the participants get back into the bucket of ice water and brought in encouragers". They were regular people, not professional Coaches who cheered them on and told them to fight through the pain.

Something remarkable happened from this small change. All the participants doubled or tripled their time in the ice bucket.

The only thing that changed in the room was encouragement. That s why this is another way to add value to a coach-client relationship. The client might have picture perfect form but you never know if they're going through a tough time at home.

They don't just need your coaching cues, they need someone to believe in them too. Encouragement is oxygen for the soul.

Moving Target

The 3 C s of Coaching are the most valuable aspects of our service. It s the actual intangibles behind why someone pays for our service. You can t touch it. But you know it s there.

If you ever have a retention problem, I guarantee that the clients aren't one or all of the 3 C s. They may have said "my schedule changed" but in reality they are saying "I haven't felt challenged."

The goal of a Coach who cares and wants to see their clients succeed is to identify which of the 3 C's your clients needs at this point in time.

It s a moving target. People are dynamic so their needs will change throughout the year.

You must be adaptable and deliver to them what they need. Deliver the 3 C's of Coaching and your clients will never question your value. They will see you as one of the best investments in their life.

Value Bomb 💣
Rate Your Coaches On The 3 C s Of Coaching

- On a Scale 1-10, Rate How Well You Correct Clients
- One a Scale 1-10, Rate How Well You Challenge Clients
- On a Scale 1-10, Rate How Well You Cheer Clients

Chapter 3

Your Ideal Customer

After you get your service dialed in, it s time to get your gym packed with ideal customers. We want to consider the demographics and psychographics of your ideal customer.

The first step is to make a list of the top 5 clients in your gym right now. What are some common themes among them?

Demographics	Psychographics
• Age	• Interests
• Gender	• Buying Behavior
• Single / Married	• Personality
• Location	• Values
• Income	• Lifestyle

Now that you have a list of the 5 clients, write down 5-10 demographic and psychographic notes next to their name.

The final component is to write down how these clients interact with your business.

- What problem did they come to you to solve?
- What do they value most about your service?
- What do they value least?
- What are common words or phrases they use to describe themselves and their goals?

When I became a Gym Owner I wanted to work with anyone and everyone. If you had goals and a heartbeat, you were a good fit for me. I ve found that to be a huge mistake when it comes to running a small service based business.

I was lacking clarity on my ideal customer.

Your ideal customer is the person that you are most gifted at serving. They bring you the most joy to work with and there's a big demand from this group of people for your service.

I ve made the mistake in the past of trying to serve too many people. I got burned out because I wasn't focusing on the type of client I want to help most. I started with boot camp for adults, then I threw in a kids program. And eventually I even tested an older adult program. It was a hot mess.

I was throwing everything at the wall and it didn't lead to growth. On top of that, I was a yes man" to session times. If at least 3-4 people requested a time, I added it to our schedule. I was running 13 sessions per day, many of them back-to-back with no break.

Again, a huge waste of time and energy because the gym didn't grow.

There's a great story that ties into this lesson...

A father and son were walking through the forest on their way to town with their donkey. They came across a group of people who said to the father "your poor son, why don't you let him rest and ride the donkey?"

The father said "you're right" and put his son on the donkey. They continued on their journey. After awhile, they ran into another group of people who said to the boy "your poor father. Don't you see he's your elder? Why don't you let him rest and ride the donkey too."

The father agreed and joined his son on the donkey. Then they came across a third group who said "that poor donkey has to carry two people on his back. Why don't you give the donkey a rest?"

The father felt guilty. So he decided that they would carry the donkey to let it rest. They tied up the donkey to a log upside down and carried it. The donkey didn't like being tied up after awhile and starting kicking around.

He made the father and son drop him near the river where the donkey fell into the water and drowned.

What's the moral of the story?

When you try to please everyone, you end up being a drowning jackass.

As Gym Owners, we can be people pleasers. That s what draws us to this line of work because we want to serve people but like many gifts, it can also be a curse.

Serving your ideal customer sounds limiting but it actually allows you to focus.

- You can speak to your ideal customer in your content.
- Your service will be built your avatars problems.
- You can spot distractions easier and say no to them.

Your goal is to be a specialist, not a generalist. Specialists get paid more (think brain surgeon vs family physician) and they get referrals because they solve a specific problem.

If your clients can t articulate the problem you solve, you are in trouble because they are the person referring.

If I interviewed your clients, which problem would they say you solve?

If you offer too many services (kickboxing, yoga, boot camp, personal training, etc) then they might say oh they do a little bit of everything." When was the last time you heard someone said Hey Mike, can you recommend any gyms that do a little bit of everything?"

That never happens!

They say things like I need to lose this gut, know any good trainers?" or my kids need more speed work for football, who s the best at that?" or I need more stretching and flexibility, what s a good yoga studio around here?"

People ask for solutions to specific problems. Own your solution and become known as the best at one thing and don t get distracted by adding more services. That makes you a me too" gym. If your gym has a schedule like the class schedule of a big box gym, you are now competing with them. And you probably have less space and a smaller budget.

A personal training studio or coaching facility wins big when they are known as the local expert to one audience with a specific problem. The riches are in the niches!

<u>Super Mario Marketing</u>

Becoming hyper specific makes your marketing 10x more powerful because it will really speak to that audience and resonate with their problems.

Now we can apply Super Mario Bros to your marketing to get you more ideal customers.

I was introduced to the concept of Super Mario Marketing by Shann Puri from the My First Million podcast. If you've ever played Super Mario Bros. then you are probably familiar with the fire flower that allows you to shoot fireballs and kick ass. How does this apply to marketing?

- Your customer is Mario.
- Your product is the Fire Flower.
- The dream outcome is Fire Mario.

Most Gym Owners are focusing on their product (the fire flower) and selling people on how awesome it is.

- We have the best workouts
- We are conveniently located
- We offer 9 sessions daily
- We have the highest energy Coaches

Notice all the language is about us and how awesome we are. The best marketing makes the customer the hero.
They shine a light on them and how their life will be improved as a result of using their product or service. They showcase how the customer will become Fire Mario.

- You will have more energy and confidence
- You will love how clothes fit on your body
- You will smirk when you see yourself in the mirror
- You will proudly wear your bathing suit
- You will get off your medications once and for all

A big switch is adding you" before each statement because it speaks to the person directly. Your reader sees the word you" but thinks to themselves me".

Make a giant list of all the life upgrades that come from a result of your service. You can do client interviews and write their words down verbatim. Your clients can often articulate the benefits better than you or me.

Your clients will use words that connect with other ideal customers who feel the same way. Add their words to your marketing and you ll see massive improvements.

To take it a step further, I highly recommend interviewing your clients on video or asking them to record a video testimonial. We've used it on ads and it's yield some of the best marketing results in recent years.

Serving Mrs. Jones

Most coaching facilities serve a customer avatar that I refer to as Mrs. Jones. She wants to lose fat after having two kids, getting married and working a desk job for years.

She s packed on 30 pounds and wants to reclaim her old body. She wants to tone up and feel more confident. She talks negatively to herself in the mirror and puts everyone else first in her life.

Do you see how many problems I can solve for this ideal customer?

- Training: Design workouts for Mrs. Jones that tones her entire body specifically her "trouble zones"
- Nutrition: Connect Mrs Jones with a meal prep company to save time and money.
- Mindset: Workshops for Mrs. Jones around negative self talk and how it impacts her goals

- Education. Teach Mrs. Jones how to read labels so she can make informed decisions to pick foods that support her goals
- Accountability: Check-in weekly with her via email, text, DM or audio message to ask about her week and how I can support her.

I m taking all her problems then building my company to be a solution machine for her. As I get to know her more I can anticipate more problems and create resources for those too.

- Dining Out Guide for those meals on-the-go
- Travel Workout Guide with bodyweight workouts and hotel gym workouts
- Movie Theater Snack Guide with a list of low sugar great tasting treats
- Healthy Holiday Swaps with high protein recipes for popular holiday dishes
- Mobility Homework Manual so she can stretch at home and loosen up tight muscles

My team and I stay fired up about helping Mrs. Jones because she is the nucleus of the household. When she gets more healthy and fit then it creates a ripple effect in the household.

When she eats better, the husband and kids eat better.

When she puts herself first and makes her health a priority, she s leading her family to do the same.

When she is strong and confident in her body, her family likes to see her smiling more.

That s why being clear on our ideal customer is so powerful. You can serve them to the highest of your ability. And charge more for it because you re an expert at serving that ideal customer.

Value Bomb 💣

Ideal Customer Exercise

- Write down the name of your top 5 clients.
- What makes them so awesome and what are common traits about them?
- What is their #1 fitness goal? (Focus on that as your primary service)
- What are your ideal customers' main pain points?
- What solutions can you create for those pain points?

Chapter 4

Offers So Good They Sell Themselves

After you get your product and experience at 10/10 and your ideal customer is identified, you can build powerful offers that speak to them. This is your customers first impression so make it remarkable.

I recommend you build two offers...

1. Signature Offer
2. Transformation Offer

Your Signature Offer is your budget friendly option for people who have a workout problem" and need more movement in their daily life. This tends to be a group training offer that allows one Coach to train many. This is also a down sell if they can t work with you in your Transformation Program.

The Transformation Offer is your red-carpet experience. It s your premium product. The second tier in your service. This is ideally for someone with a workout and nutrition problem". Also, it could include more exclusive training like small group or one-on-one.

The Signature Offer solves one problem and the Transformation Offer solves more problems, hence the price difference.

I don t want to create blanket pricing for these offers but here s price examples....

- **Signature Offer: $149-$199/month**
  Includes boot camp training only

- **Transformation Offer: $299-$499/month**
  Includes assigned Coach, small group training, nutrition coaching, weekly check-ins and monthly InBody scan.

Some people just want to workout and have zero interest in getting help with nutrition. Others want help with workouts and nutrition but need to be charged accordingly.

In the fitness industry, we tend to give away the house for too little. All that ends up happening is the client doesn t value your time or the service you re providing. Nutrition coaching is an entirely separate level of service. But most Gym Owners add it into their boot camp membership and get frustrated when compliance is low.

Sometimes it s because the client simply doesn t want help with nutrition. You can t force it on them. But you can earn their trust over time and educate them on the importance of nutrition changes. And if finances are the issue, don't lose hope.

A "no" is really a not right now. Their situation could change down the road.

When a client is ready to commit, you must charge them appropriately for the extra time investment you will be making in their success. Reviewing their nutrition tracking, biofeedback and progress takes time and specialty skills. There must be an added charge for that.

Pricing Is Everything

Most Gym Owners pick their pricing based on what others are charging. Instead of doing that, let's take a moment to reimagine your business.

If you had a clean slate, what would you charge to service your clients at the highest level?

Charging more isn't a bad thing. You're not being a greedy business owner. You are after true transformation in your clients and that requires using every weapon at your disposal.

Some Gym Owners will take jabs at gyms who charge more or less than them. They don't understand they are in the worst spot possible.

If another gym is priced lower, they will say...

"Don't go to that cheap $10/mo gym down the street, you get what you pay for."

If another gym is priced higher, they will say...

"Don't go to that pricey personal training studio, they charge an arm and a leg."

What they don't understand is that in business there's the cheapest and there's the best. Everything in the middle is where the struggle exists.

The cheapest is usually the worst experience because they don t have any margins. They cross their fingers that their low prices will one day bring volume but it never comes. And they either struggle to stay open and eventually close up shop.

I'm not pointing fingers at anyone because I've made the mistake of charging too little. In fact, my first boot camp gym was $99/month for unlimited sessions. A small percentage of my clients were getting result. Their attendance was hit-or-miss and they rarely followed my nutrition advice.

When I raised my rates, my clients got better results, attendance skyrocketed and I saw more nutrition compliance. It taught me a powerful lesson.

The more you pay the more you pay attention.

I didn t change my coaching approach. The higher price attracted a serious client who followed my marching orders. I want to hammer this point home because this one topic causes so much stress for Gym Owners. It all stems from one decision - pricing.

I don t want you to get burned out or have paper thin profit margins.

That s why I'm on a mission to spread the good news that you can take your business back by changing your pricing. It takes courage but it s worth it. You will re-spark your passion when you are charging what you are worth.

Alex Hormozi says the following happens when you charge more...
- *The More Someone Pays, The More Invested They Are*
- *The More Invested They Are, The Better Results They Get*
- *The Better Results They Get, The More Convicted The Sales Team Is*

- *The More Convicted The Sales Team Is, The More Sales They Make*
- *The More Sales They Make, The More Profit We Have*
- *The More Profit We Have, The More We Can Invest Back Into Client Success*

Here's what Hormozi says happens when you charge less...

- *The Less You Pay, The Less Invested They Are*
- *The Less Invested They Are, The Worse Results They GetThe Worse Results They Get, The Less Convicted The Sales Team Is*
- *The Less Convicted The Sales Team Is, The Fewer Sales They Make*
- *They Fewer Sales They Make, The Less Profit We Have*
- *The Less Profit We Have, The Less We Have to Invest into Client Success*

I want to say this again - **pricing is everything!**

It will dictate how invested the client will be in your program and how invested you are in their success.

⬤ Stop giving your time away for free, you are too valuable.

⬤ Stop charging $1/day, it tells the client you don't value your time.

⬤ Stop discounting your service, you are more valuable than a doctor.

⬤ Stop thinking fitness is "just a workout" because you save lives. The fitness industry has struggled for long enough from a negative money mindset. We charge too little, give too much of ourselves and we are not winning the war against obesity.

Something has to change and I want you to see the power of pricing. Raising your prices is the best thing you can do for yourself, your family, your team and your clients.

Charging too little puts everyone in a world of hurt.

Client success begins at the price! So charge more!

Guarantees

There s risk in every transaction. The company holds some and the customer holds some. If you re confident in your service, you would bear the majority of the risk and remove as much as possible from the client.

This is your 300th time taking someone through a transformation. This is their first. Doesn t it make sense you remove the risk since you re the expert in the transaction?

A guarantee gives someone a sense of security and safety to move forward with the transaction. By simply adding a guarantee you can add an extra 20-30% to your closing percentage.

From the buyer's perspective, they have little or nothing to lose. You can even offer to put it in writing on a legally binding contract so they know it s all legit. Before, I said the client needs to put their money where their mouth is. This is where you do the same.

You can add a Conditional Guarantee that states if you do x then I will give you x.

Here s a few examples of a Conditional Guarantee…

- If you do x and don t reach your goal by the deadline, I will refund 100% of your money
- If you do x and don t reach your goal by the deadline, I will train you for free until you do
- If you do x and don t reach your goal by the deadline, I will DOUBLE YOUR MONEY in membership credit

The conditions are what you deem as absolutely necessary for the person to be successful. It could be a certain amount of workouts or nutrition tracking to meet your conditions. If they do it, they win by having a leaner, healthier body. If they fail to meet the conditions, the guarantee is voided.
Pick things that are simple and trackable. It should be something you can measure easily, otherwise, you will have headaches.

The Unconditional Guarantee has no conditions. But it could be a window of time they need to speak up. Maybe it s a 90 day Unconditional Guarantee that states if they're not happy for any reason, they can ask for a refund.

Again, if you are confident in your skills and the service you provide, these guarantees shouldn t scare you. Costco dominates their competition because of their world famous guarantee.

Here s the Costco guarantee..

Costco has a 100% risk-free satisfaction guarantee on its membership and merchandise. If you are not satisfied with either for any reason, you can request a refund or replace the item.

You can return an item if you don't want it anymore, you bought it by mistake, you're not happy with it or there's an issue. And you don't even need a receipt or original packaging. It's a crazy awesome guarantee!!

That s why so many people choose to make big purchases at Costco. They know they are protected by their amazing guarantee.

Costco stock value has doubled in the last 5 years. They have high team retention and strong profit margins. It's safe to say they outsell what they lose in returns and refunds. That's a powerful guarantee worth adding to your offer!

Bonuses
Gym Owners are humble folks and that means they have a hard time bragging about their services. We tend to think of what we

offer as a bundle but that bites you in the butt. It tells the client you don t value everything you do.

I want to encourage you to point out every single thing you've built for your service.

Most Gym Owners say they offer workouts, nutrition and accountability. It s not very powerful to say 3 words and expect the client to understand the value.

You have to unpack it and let them know what you offer and the bonuses that solve problems beyond the workouts.

🎁 Bonus #1: Kick In The Pants" Accountability System To Make Sure You Workout 3x Week

🎁 Bonus #2: Monthly In-Body Scan So You Can See Your Metabolism Go Up

🎁 Bonus #3: Travel Workout Guide So You Have a Coach On The Road

🎁 Bonus #4: Dining Out Guide So You Know Which Menu Items Help You Hit Your Goals

I recommend a printed price sheet with a side-by-side comparison of your Signature Offer and Transformation Offer.

Most fitness professionals prefer to have printed materials in their hands. Create easy-to-use tools that help them communicate your programs and pricing. A simple pricing sheet can look like this....

Value Bomb 💣

Create Your Offers

- What type of service are you most passionate about offering to your customers?
- What do you include in your program?
  (List them out and give them a catchy name)
- What guarantee can enhance your offer?
- What bonuses can you pack in to add more value?
- What pricing allows you to serve at the highest level and gets your clients to pay attention?

Chapter 5

How To Get Infinite Leads

When you look at your business, think of it like a water hose. The water enters on one side and moves along to the other end. That s how clients move through their experience with your business.

It looks like this...

Step #1 - Lead Generation (they see your ads)

Step #2 - Lead Nurture (they are contacted by your team)

Step #3 - Conversion (they are sold your services)

Step #4 - Fulfillment (they are given coaching)

Step #5 - Retention & Ascension (they stay and move up to higher services)

This is also the order you want to troubleshoot your business. The first part of the hose is lead generation. You can't stress test the rest of the hose until you have strong lead flow.

To help you get that flow, I've listed 10 of my best lead generation strategies so we can get you more leads than you've ever had before and can move on to the other areas of the hose. Below are my top paid and organic marketing strategies.

PAID MARKETING

#1) Facebook and Instagram Ads

At this time, running ads on these platforms is still the biggest bang for your buck. Every market is different and requires testing to find what works. That s the marketing game.

Too many Gym Owners throw in the towel after 2-3 tests and say Facebook Ads don t work". But they need to be more resilient to how marketing works.

It s only a failure if you don t learn from it. Take the failed campaigns as a learning lesson getting you closer to find what is working.

I recommend at least $30/day in ad spend to see meaningful results. If you need a good marketing agency, send me a DM and I can point you to one. I know many so if you tried one and weren t happy, I can point you to another.

DM me at facebook.com/DustinBogle or IG @dustin.bogle

If you are running ads and seeing a strong lead flow, then the next part of the hose to troubleshoot is lead nurture. I will go into this more in Section II: Sales Multipliers

In my experience, your leads fall into 3 main categories...

1. Lay Downs - they ve heard about you and are ready to buy, they are reaching out to say take my money". You don t need to be a skilled salesperson to collect their cash.

2. Not Right Now - these are the hard no s" but don t give up on them. A no is just a not right now". They re not in a season of focusing on their health so don t waste your time trying to force them. It s a losing battle.

3. Fence Riders - this where salesmanship comes in. They are one foot in and one foot out. They have doubts and fears that your program will work. You need to get in contact with them and show them why you're a good fit for them. That s why it s so important you talk to them on the phone because they need to hear your energy, tone and compassion.

That s why I created Gym Reinforcements - so we can reach out to your leads over the phone and sell them your offer.

#2) Giveaway Ads

This is a variation of the first marketing strategy. One of the best ways to surge your list is to give something away for free. It can be a membership giveaway, challenge giveaway or free meal plan. We ve seen recording-breaking lead flow when a gym runs a free giveaway. After all, who doesn't like to win free stuff?

Now you need to get creative on how you can spin it so the leads can be presented with a paid offer. One of my favorite ways to do this is to give away 4 free spots in a 28 Day Challenge. Each week, you can pick one winner and legitimately give them a free challenge so you have 4 winners per month.

After you draw the grand prize winner, text the other optins that they won the second place prize - a 50% off promo code.

But add urgency by mentioning it's only active for the next 72 hours.

From there you can blame the ticking clock about why they need to respond ASAP and why you are aggressively reaching out. You can reach out and say CONGRATS! You won our second place prize. I wanted to get a hold of you before your prize expires in 72 hours. Are you free to chat or is tomorrow better?"

#3) Signage

This is another great form of advertising. Most Gym Owners set up their signage once and forget about it. You should rotate banners or yard stake signs throughout the year to catch the eyes of drivers. When you drive by the same shopping center everyday, it becomes a blur and you don t pay attention to them anymore.

Shake things up. Put up a big attention grabbing banner 2x a year when you are running a big challenge to encourage walk-ins. You can add your phone number or social media too. Pro tip - don't put dates on the banner so it s evergreen and can be used every year.

#4) Referral Contests

Select a two week timeframe for your members to compete on bringing in referrals for a chance to win a prize. We ve done mountain bikes, Apple watches, TVs and other cool stuff.

Put the prize in the gym with a big red bow so your clients are reminded about it at every session. You will always make back the cost of your prize if you promote it hard.

If a member refers someone to your program, they get a ticket into the drawing. The more referrals they send, the more chances they have to win. Give them some coaching on who to look for (people who are struggling with weight loss) and how to invite them to the gym. You could even write them a templated post on their social media. Remove the friction and make it easy on them.

#5) Local Business Affiliate Deals

Selling one-off memberships is like fishing for trout. Going into a business and landing multiple sales is like harpooning a whale. One of the best ways to do that is to brainstorm a list of local businesses that have the same ideal customer as you.

Businesses like hair salons, tanning salons, chiropractors, massage therapists and physical therapists. Think health and beauty industry.

After you make a list, you want to approach them with an amazing deal for their staff. Give them a special deal since they will be talking about you to their customers from experience. There s nothing like having a hair stylist that's getting fit with you and talking about it up to her clients. That word-of-mouth marketing is worth giving them a discounted membership or commission.

The best way to get the attention of a local business is to be the person coming in with unexpected gifts. One of the best strategies I used in the past was coming in with a plate of cookies and a signup sheet. It read at the top when you are ready to work these off, I d love to have you train with me at my personal training facility. Text me at this number to learn how you can train with me for ½ off."

#6) Chamber of Commerce

The investment to join your local Chamber of Commerce is well worth it. It's an opportunity to stand in front of high net-worth individuals that live in your local area. And they have customers and a team they can point to you as well. It's a great move on your part to get to know these people and build a relationship.

When you join the Chamber of Commerce you get a free 5 minute introduction to share who you are and what your business you are in.

This is a golden opportunity to sell B2B. You can explain that you know about the struggles of being a busy business owner. And how it's easy to put your health on the back burner. Then make them an offer.

When I joined the Chamber of Commerce, I offered them a chamber member discount. When the meeting was over, 12 business owners gave me their business cards and asked me to sign them up. Harpooning whales baby!

ORGANIC MARKETING

#7) Social Media Content

You can get plenty of leads from putting out great content. It must be informative, entertaining and shareable. Get together with your team and have fun filming videos in your gym.

Make a list of questions you get from your members and take a moment to teach but make it info-tainment. People go to social media to tune out from their daily life and get entertained.

Give your best fat-loss advice on social media so you can grow your audience. Show them your best hacks on how to live a healthy lifestyle. And sprinkle in storytelling. You can tell your story and your clients' story. Drop a call-to-action in your posts so they know what to do next if they're interested in working with you. This doesn t cost money, it only costs time.

#8) Convo Starter Posts

This is a subcategory of the previous topic but it s worth mentioning. These posts where you ask your audience to engage by commenting. It s usually 1-2 sentences and speaks to the reader about a specific topic or problem they have.

If they go to your profile and see you are an expert around this topic, they will engage.

A couple of examples are…

- *Who wants to lose 20+ pounds by working with a trainer?*

- *Who needs more accountability and support to reach their fitness goals?*

- *I m looking for 5 ladies to go through a transformation program? Comment if interested.*

These work like a charm but don t overdo them. A Convo Starter can be posted on your profile or stories. And another great spot to find leads that is often overlooked is local FB groups.

I m talking about the local moms running group or the buy/sell/trade group or the what's happening in x city group. They often have thousands of local residents. And if are active and add value, you can find a steady flow of potential customers.

I was able to keep my calendar 100% full for months with no paid ads.

My daily routine was simple...

- Post convo starters in 3-4 local FB groups every night at 8-9pm.
- I'd get 30-50 comments and half would reply to my DMs.
- I booked the DM into sales appointments for the next day.

Like anything, this only works if you work it!

#9) Friends and Family Week

This is a simple and easy concept that costs zero dollars. Plan a week where your members can bring their friends and family to your sessions for free. They can take as many workouts as they want but they have to fill out a waiver beforehand.

That means you need their name, phone and email. It's a great way to get more leads from your members. And they will be the most qualified too since your members pre-sell them on your awesome service.

#10) FB / IG Deep Dive

This is another strategy that costs nothing but time. If you ve been open for years then you probably have a inbox with a deep history of messages. Some of them led to a sale but some of them dropped off and went unresponsive.

Doing a "deep dive" involves going back through your inbox history and reactivating those cold convos. A great ice breaker is "hey, I haven't got a chance to get in contact with you. Are you still looking for help with your fitness goals?" I recommend doing this every 8-12 weeks.

BONUS: MINING FOR GOLD

These are bonus strategies to wake up" your sleeping database of leads. If you have thousands of leads from past marketing efforts, these tips will move those folks into a sale.

Text Blasts

I m shocked at how many Gym Owners who do not use text blasts on a regular basis. They have an even bigger response rate than emails. I have a full assault plan for you to use in the next section so I won t spend too much time on this right now.

First things first, if you don t have a text service then get one ASAP. I recommend Fit Pro Tracker or High Level.

The simplest way to get people to respond to a text blast is to ask questions about them. It has to be written like it came from a friend. If it's too formal it will hurt your response rate.

Here s some of our best performing scripts, look how simple they....
Hey [name]...do you still need support with your fitness goals?

Quick question for your [name].....are you free to workout in the mornings or evenings?

Hey, it's Coach Dustin and I'm gathering some data. What do you struggle with most [name]...workouts or nutrition?

[name], I'm looking for 5 women to go through a Pilot Program that will require 3 workouts and you must follow my meal plan. Interested?

Send these out to your old leads and watch the responses come in. Then use my follow up system (covered in an upcoming chapter) to convert them into a sale.

Reactivate Past Members

When was the last time you personally called your past members to check in on them? Reach out and find out how things have been going in their life. They will almost always go into "fitness confessional" and share how they fell off the wagon and need your help.

Your past members know, like and trust you. They know where your gym is located, they know the rates and they are some of the easiest people to sell.

Make it fun and interesting. One of the quickest and easiest ways to follow up with past members is to batch shoot personalized videos and text them out.

Hey Sarah!! I miss you!! How are you doing? Are you sticking to your workout habit?

BOOM!! That makes you stand out among the competition and follow up in a way that no one is doing it. Again, this takes time but it s well worth it. I recommend doing it quarterly.

Email Marketing

Although this is paid marketing, it is very inexpensive. One of my favorite email marketing systems is iContact because it has a high inbox rate. You can t get people to read your email if you don t land in their inbox. One of the first things you should build in your email marketing automation is a Trust Building Campaign.

I mentioned how you have lay downs, not right now s and fence riders.

The Trust Building Campaign will help you to cover the fence riders by bridging the gap between I don t know who you are" to I'm interested in working with you."

Trust = Transactions

When trust is not established, the person will simply not buy from you. Ask yourself this question…when is the last time you followed someone on social media and bought something the same day.

I bet that's never happened. Yet, Gym Owners expect their leads to buy from them the same day they optin. Unless they are a lay down, that just isn't going to happen.

Is it fair to say that s an unrealistic expectation from them and your marketing agency? It s on you (the gym owner) to build trust with those leads and the Trust Building Campaign is an automated way to do that.

Here's an overview of the Trust Building Campaign…

Day 1: Meet The Owner: Explain Why You Opened The Gym (ALTERNATE VERSION: Meet the Manager / Head Coach and Why They Chose To Work at This Gym)

Day 2: Share Your Proven Process and Who You Help (Ideal Customer)

Day 3: Share a Client Testimonial #1

Day 5: Share a Client Testimonial #2

Day 7: Share a Fitness or Fat-Loss Myth You Used to Believe (Makes You Relatable)
Day 9: Explain Details of Signature Offer with Call-To-Action

Day 10: Shorter Recap of Signature Offer with Call-To-Action

Now we took the trust building process that could have taken a month and compressed it into two weeks. Don t get me wrong, you should absolutely reach out to your leads and offer your service after you get a new optin.

But if they are not responding, then you should drop them into your Trust Building Campaign and reach out afterward.

Value Bomb 💣

Marketing Feedback

- What is your best paid and organic marketing strategy?
- Which paid marketing strategy do you want to add next?
- Which organic marketing strategy do you want to add next?
- Who will own that marketing strategy? You or someone else on your team?
- Do you have a trust building campaign setup? If not, build one ASAP

SECTION II

SALES MULTIPLIERS

Chapter 6

The Convicted Lawyer

There was a man who was required to pay his traffic ticket at the local town courthouse. He loved TV shows like Law & Order, so he decided it was a good opportunity to see the legal system in action, and try to find a courtroom with a juicy case.

The next day, he went to the courthouse and paid his traffic ticket and then stepped into a nearby courtroom. He took a seat and noticed that this case was near the end because they were wrapping up with closing arguments.

The Defense Attorney was defending his client who was accused of murder. It was time for final remarks, and the lawyer could sense that the jury was not on their side.

He knew he had to throw a Hail Mary at them.

The Defense Attorney stood up in front of the jury and said his closing statement.

Ladies and gentlemen of the jury! My client is innocent. He s been wrongfully accused of murder and the evidence is clear he never did it. In fact, I know this to be true because in 60 seconds, the person he was accused of murdering will walk through those courtroom doors. He pointed to the back of the courtroom.

The jury was shocked he would make such a claim. They began to murmur and talk amongst one another. The judge slammed his gavel and declared *Order in the court! Please allow him to finish his statement."*

All heads turned to the Defense Attorney who was standing tall with his arm up extended and his index finger pointing at the courtroom doors. The jurors look at the clock then the front door.

He claimed the person that was murdered would walk through the doors in 60 seconds. Now it s time to wait and see.

10 seconds goes by. The jurors were watching the doors like a hawk.
20 seconds goes by. The jurors begin to look at one another.

40 seconds goes by. The jurors leaned to the edge of their seats.

57....58....59 seconds.....here it comes!

After a minute, no one walked through the door.

Heads turned to the lawyer who began his next statement.
Ladies and gentlemen. The law indicates that if you have a shadow of a doubt in my client's guilt then you must vote not guilty . All of you looked at the courtroom door which tells me that you believed there was a chance that the person my client is accused of murdering might walk through those doors. You ve demonstrated your doubt. Now, do what is right, and come back with a not guilty verdict. Thank you for your time.

The lawyer sat down and the jury went to the deliberation room. A short time later they came back to the courtroom with a verdict. The jury foreman read, *We have come to a verdict and, we the jury, find the defendant guilty....*"

Before the foreman can finish, the lawyer jumped up and said, *WHAT?!! You all looked at the door. That s proof you had doubt. How could you vote guilty?!*"

That s when the jury foreman said *You are right. We did look at the courtroom doors and you did have us doubting at that moment. But we looked at you and your client. And you were not looking at the doors, which is how we knew he was guilty."*

Wow!! What a powerful story. It demonstrates that our conviction, or lack of conviction, is contagious. Humans are remarkable at sniffing out a fraud.

People don t need to believe what we are saying.
They believe that **we believe** in what we are saying.

Conviction is built through belief in yourself, your team and your process.

I know how to Coach people because I ve done it for over two decades. I firmly believe in my team because we have A-players who really care about our clients and we ve made our process simple, so it can be easily taught and scaled.

If you are not convicted, then it s time to improve your product so you feel fired up about getting it out into the world. You don t want to be the lawyer that says all the right things" but doesn t back it up with their actions.

If you don t feel immensely convicted in what you are selling, it will greatly hurt your conversions. Maybe in the back of your mind you aren t confident in your product because you haven t produced a before-and-after transformation in months.

That means it's time to strap on your boots and make your product better. Find the weak links and improve them so you can feel convicted in selling it. Add more accountability, ask for feedback from your members on what you can do better, create a member challenge so you can give a small group of clients more attention and get them amazing results.

You want to feel proud that the prospects get to purchase this program because it will change their life. If you are not fired up about selling it, then strengthening the product is the quickest way to get you more convicted.

The second thing you can do is read your 5-star reviews. We can be our biggest critic and pick apart what s wrong with our service. But when you read your reviews, you can get a quick reminder of the changes you created for your clients.

Selling someone saves them because you are putting them in a program that has the highest chance of success - a coaching program.

Coaches create physical change, but I m preaching to the choir when I list all the ripple effects that come from getting healthy and fit.

- More confidence
- Higher all-day energy
- Revved up metabolism

- Strength and endurance
- Improved mental health and mood
- Managed blood sugar and insulin
- Sharper thinking, learning and decision making
- Reduced risk of lifestyle disease (cancer, heart disease, diabetes)
- Healthy outlet for stress
- Improved sexual health (to do horizontal hula as The Rock calls it)
- Longer and better quality of life

The real question is that if you are going to offer all these benefits to someone, what is a fair price?

The answer is that your health doesn t have a dollar amount. It s priceless.

Anyone who has lost their health will tell you they will pay anything to get it back.

And the best way for them to take their health back is to hire a Coach. An expert who will pour their knowledge into them and be their guide along their journey.

You can tell I m convicted in selling coaching.....are you?

Value Bomb 💣

Rate Your Conviction

- Read 5-10 of your client reviews from Google, FB or Yelp

- On a scale 1-10, rate your conviction about helping others to get healthy and fit
- On a scale 1-10, rate your teams conviction
- How can you tell someone is convicted to help others to get healthy and fit?

Chapter 7

The Fortune Follow Up System

If you've studied sales then you've probably heard the phrase **"the fortune is in the follow up"**.

I believe in that so much that I created a company that obsesses on that critical area of a business, Gym Reinforcements, where we do 100% of your lead follow up and sales with a dedicated Sales Associate trained by us.

But I'm going to pull back the curtain and reveal exactly what we do with our lead follow up because I want you to be successful, regardless if you work with us or not.

The Fortune Follow Up system is a unique and highly effective way to get more sales from your current lead flow and sleeping database of contacts.

This is the exact system that helped me go from a stressed-out Gym Owner wearing all the hats and bringing in $10,000/month to an absentee Gym Owner with a million dollar company doing over $100,000/month.

The Fortune Follow Up System is broken into 4 parts…

1. **Hire a Professional Sales Associate**
2. **Execute The Black Belt Basics**
3. **Create a Daily Feedback Loop**
4. **Evaluate The Numbers**

But before we dive into who, what, when and how….let's start with why.

Why do we need aggressive follow up?
Why aren't they just throwing money at us?

There's quite a few reasons, but the biggest reason is that people are extremely busy, distracted and overwhelmed with information. They are getting hit all day with pings, rings and zings from texts, emails, social media, push notifications, alarms and calendar reminders - not to mention the faster pace of life outside of technology.

You need to stand out among the noise. I've had multiple people thank me for constantly following up because they are so busy. They would say, "I saw your call but I was in a meeting." or "I read your text but my kids were asking for dinner and I lost track of time."

They are being bombarded on two fronts - online and in-person.

Your follow up shouldn't be coming from a place of "Give me your money." That's when it feels like we are nagging. Instead, it should come from "I'm on a mission to help people and you reached out to me." Remember, you have the person's number because they opted in or contacted you. Now you are just getting back to them!

If you're not following up with your leads then you're showing them "I don't care about you". You can see why I get fired up about this topic.

It's not just the fortune that is in the follow up in terms of sales for your business. The fortune of a brand new life is on the line for the prospect.

Here's a great reframe that helped me to switch my mindset from it being about money to being about impact.

Leads = Lives
Sales = Saves

Every lead who expresses interest in your program is a soul. It's a person that is drowning. Their head is below water and their hand is above the water, and they are waving their hand at you asking for help.

Your marketing is like a ship passing by, and when they reach out they are asking for help. If you can get them into your program, it's like throwing them a life ring. When you sell them, you save them.

Sometimes people think you are the Director of a Cruise Ship. Planning fun events for your clients, dressing up for silly theme workouts and decorating the gym. It's important to have fun. But your main role is to be the Captain of a Battleship that's on a mission with a clear enemy that you want to destroy.

That enemy is products and services that cause people to waste their time and money without results. Stupid crap like detox teas, fat burning pills, useless home equipment, waist trimmers, starvation diets, Coaches that give our industry a bad name and gyms that give you access to equipment but don't really care if you get results.

If you truly believe in your program then you would look at every sale as a save.

That's why it's critical that you deploy the Fortune Follow Up System. There are thousands of lives in your community that need your help. Get them through your doors and save them.

#1) Hire a Professional Sales Associate

This is a hard truth - **most gyms have weak follow up.**

Here's why...the person doing the follow up doesn't love it. When you don't love something, it comes through in your performance. If you are not strong in sales, then it's highly unlikely you will train a great salesperson. If that is a punch in the gut, then I want to let you know that I've made the same mistake and it cost me millions in revenue.

Here's what we did in the past for our lead follow up....

- At first, I asked a **Coach** to do lead follow up. They didn't love it, but said "yes" to be a team player. The quality suffered because they didn't love doing it and the hours they were available to reach out were the hours the prospects aren't available. Lesson learned.

- After that, I hired an **Admin** to do follow up, but they always did their admin tasks first and follow up last. That's a clue into what people enjoy doing. They will always procrastinate on the stuff they don't enjoy. Again, my fault for giving the task to someone who doesn't love sales.

- And then there's the **Owner** who typically falls into one of two camps...
  - They crush it at sales and it's one of their natural strengths.
  - They dislike sales and it drains their energy to talk to people and ask for money.

But the Owner can't do it forever. They have to delegate and elevate if they want to grow the business. They must move around and relieve tension wherever it exists in the business, but if it's not their strength, they must hand it off as quickly as possible to a trained professional.

The million dollar lesson I learned was when I hired a dedicated Sales Rep that was obsessed with sales and loved the thrill of the hunt. They loved connecting with people, sharing how our program can help solve their problems and got into sales because it played to their strengths.

We saw a 3x increase in trial sales the first month I hired a dedicated Sales Associate to do my outreach to leads.

If I did that 5 years earlier, I could have brought in millions more in revenue across my locations. That's a painful thought but one that I want to save you from.

Hiring a Sales Associate was a big success for multiple reasons...

- It was their strength. They applied to do sales. I wasn't trying to Frankenstein roles have a Coach or Admin do sales.

- They work from home. No distractions compared to the gym.

- They could focus on dialing-for-dollars, it's their only role.

- They are better at lead management and knowing where everyone is in the pipeline.

- They study sales and want to improve their craft daily.

#2) Execute The Black Belt Basics

Once I hired a dedicated Sales Associate, I could move on to giving them a system that works. It needed to be simple because simplicity scales and complexity fails.

That's when I created The Black Belt Basics, which acts as a checklist of systems that the Sales Associate must complete daily to be successful at lead follow up. These are the exact systems we teach our team at Gym Reinforcements.

The Black Belt Basics are….

- **The 5x2 Follow Up System**
- **The 10% Prospect System**
- **The Daily 50 System**
- **The Trial Duplication System**

Let's start with the 5x2 follow up system.

The longer a lead goes without being contacted, the colder they get and the higher chance that they will start contacting other gyms. Speed to lead is a huge factor.

Most gyms have one automation or they text the lead once and give up. You have to do more than that if you want to grow your business!

Here's how the 5x2 Follow Up System works...

Day 1: Text in the Afternoon, Call in the Evening
Day 2: Text in the Afternoon, Call in the Evening
Day 3: Text in the Afternoon, Call in the Evening
Day 4: Text in the Afternoon, Call in the Evening
Day 5: Text in the Afternoon, Call in the Evening

I told you it's simple. Text them in the afternoon, call them every evening. 5 days with 2 contacts a day, that's the 5x2 Follow Up System.

The morning time is usually a mad dash for working professionals, business owners and busy moms getting their kids to school. They don't have time to respond in the morning.

In the afternoons, things quiet down a little and most people can respond to a quick text. They might be out running errands, taking a lunch break or checking their phone in the restroom. Just keeping it real. #ScrollOnTheBowl

Then in the evening when people are home from work they tend to have more time to chat and can hop on a phone call.

This is a pattern I learned from years of experiences and thousands of reach outs myself. Follow the 5x2 follow up system to convert your newest leads to a trial ASAP.
The 10% Prospect System is a clean way to reach out to old contacts in your database. If you have 1,000 or 2,000 or 5,000 contacts, it's hard to know where to begin and it can be costly to message all of them at once.

So, we created the 10% Prospect System which is where you carve out only 10% of the list and text them daily. If your Sales Associate is working 5 days per week they will get through the list every 2 weeks which means the entire list gets a text 2x month, which is a great cadence.

The Daily 50 is about making 50 outbound calls per day. We start with the newest leads on our spreadsheet and work backward. Talking to your prospects on the phone is the fastest way to build rapport, learn about their problems and present your program.

Once you get someone on the phone, you don't want to drop the ball, which is why it's important your Sales Associate is prepared for anticipated responses and the wild cards that some people will throw at you.

The last part of the Black Belt Basics is the Trial Duplication System.
This comes down to building a habit at the end of your sales calls. It's 100% free and all you have to do is ask one question.

Let's set the table....

- You've just sold a trial program or challenge. HOORAY!
- You got the client setup with everything they need to begin.
- You're about to wrap up the call but you say this line...

OMG Sarah!! I'm so excited to have you in our program. This is going to change your life and I can't wait for you to work with our team.

But you know something...we've noticed that new folks who get started with a buddy, tend to have a higher success rate.

It's probably because working out with a buddy makes you feel more comfortable and you can keep each other accountable. Do you know anyone who would like to do this challenge with you?

BOOM!!

We see an average of 3 out of 10 trial clients who will give us a referral right there on the spot. Those are free leads, you just need to ask and make it a habit to ask. You're welcome.

#3) Create a Daily Feedback Loop

This is very hard for most entrepreneurs. They like freedom and don't like to be committed to a recurring meeting. But meetings are very beneficial for your team. They typically work better with routine and structure. They need a planned time where they can talk and discuss issues.

Creating a short, daily huddle with your sales team is important because it allows for faster feedback loops. You'll want to do a role play with them, read through 1-2 sample chat flows and offer coaching and feedback. The faster they get feedback from you, the faster they can improve.

If you give feedback weekly, you are restricting your team to weekly improvements. You see how daily huddle can be valuable?

Don't make the agenda too complicated. It can be as simple as 4 key topics…

1. Wins in the last 24 hours
2. Mock call or objection overcome
3. Chat flow review (feedback on screenshots of DMs or texts)
4. Goals for the day

Keep it between 15-20 minutes and go off and crush the day. If you have to manage your own sales people, this is something you must do on your own. We do this internally for all of our Sales Associates at Gym Reinforcements so Gym Owners don't have to worry about doing this on their own.

#4) Evaluate The Numbers

This was something I dragged my feet on for way too long. I thought I could out sell my losses and just force my way to growth. That was a big mistake.

Knowing your numbers allows you to be a better business owner because you can make intelligent decisions. You might hear people sharing the 10-20 numbers they track, and that can be intimidating if you are tracking zero numbers.

That's why I recommend you get started with the basics, then add more numbers over time. It's like adding more weight to the barbell as you build your muscles.

Here's the Core 10 Metrics to begin tracking today...

- Leads
- Trials / Challenges Sold
- Membership Conversion %
- Memberships Sold
- Membership Drops
- EFT Added
- EFT Lost
- EFT Net Change
- Total Members
- Retention or Attrition %

These are critical numbers that give you feedback on what areas of your business need attention. You can quickly see if you are slowing down with lead flow, getting new folks through the doors, converting to membership or retaining your clients. Now you know where to deploy resources and spend your time as the business owner.

Do you see why it's so important for you to get low-level tasks off your plate? You are best serving your clients, your team and your business when you can have a moment to breathe and look at your numbers.

A trained Sales Associate should be able to enter these numbers for you each week so you can look at the trends week-by-week and spot the patterns.

Now you can see the power behind the Fortune Follow Up System. It's 4 core systems that build off each other and they are meant to free up your time so you can work *on* the business, not *in* the business.

Value Bomb 💣

Evaluate the Fortune Follow Up System in your business:

- Do you have a dedicated Sales Associate owning lead follow up?
- Are they executing the Black Belt Basics daily? (5x2 Follow Up, 10% Prospect Text, 50 Outbound Calls, Trial Duplication System)
- Do you have a Daily Huddle to deliver feedback quickly?
- Are you tracking your Core 10 metrics?

Chapter 8

The C.H.A.R.M Sales Process

I was on a selling spree and these are days you don't want to end. You want to contact as many people as possible because you feel like you can close anyone. I was just wrapping up a big paid-in-full deal worth over $3,000. One of my teammates overheard that conversation and said, "Dustin, you are really great at closing people with charm."

She was absolutely right. Sometimes you need outside eyes to better understand yourself. One of my strengths when selling is doing it from a place of wanting to solve the other person's problems and not being afraid to ask for the sale. After all, great service costs money to deliver it.

I took a hard look at how I do my sales calls and broke it into a simple acronym - C.H.A.R.M.

Follow these steps to add more C.H.A.R.M to your sales process and you won't feel slimy, salesy, pushy or desperate.

Those are all turn offs and it will cost you in the long run since people will tell 10 friends when they have a negative experience.

Crack a Smile

My first goal when talking to a prospect is to get a smile or laugh within the first 10-30 seconds. I usually open with something funny about myself and I'm definitely showing a big smile from the start. I want them to see I take what I do seriously, but I don't take myself too seriously. It might be something funny that happened to me that day or a funny observation. I want them to know they can feel at ease and this will be a casual conversation among friends, not a stiff sales presentation.

How Can I Help?

After they are smiling and I can read that they are comfortable, I want to find out about their problems. I want to get to know about the prospects' goals and what they want to achieve, fitness wise. At this point I like to take notes to show them that they are important. One of the best ways to make someone feel important is to make sure they feel understood. You don't want to incorrectly repeat back what they said. That will make them feel misunderstood. You want to repeat back their goals in their words - verbatim.

Ask For Details

Now you want to collect the juicy details. Don't start at just the surface level problems. Ask for more details so they can feel the pain at a deeper level and you can better understand it. You want to ask questions with "feel" in them.

- How does that extra weight make you feel?
- How long have you been feeling that way?
- When you bought that program at the other gym and it didn't work, how did it make you feel?
- How do you want to feel in your body right now?
- Do you have any physical pain every day?

The more details you have, the better. Most people will make a quick decision when you only collect surface level information.

The deeper you go on details, the more connection you have, and the higher chance of closing them since you are likely the first gym to get to know them with thorough intake questions before pitching.

Most gyms are just pitching so this will separate you.

Reveal Your Solution

This is the part in the sale where you want to get really excited and have high energy. The big reveal is coming, and there should be a major uptick in enthusiasm.

First off, you should recap what they shared with you in terms of their goals. Use as many details and "feeling statements" as possible to really heighten the pain and urgency to solve this problem.

Next, you must build immense value. Seriously aim to build 5x the value in your pitch. If you charge $299/month then you need to build value as if this service costs $1,500/month before you reveal your solution.

This part of the process is critical because, if you do an excellent job of communicating the value, the sale is a slam dunk. Rush through this portion and you will get objections.

The final step is to reveal your solution. Based on the clients goals it could be your Signature Offer or Transformation Offer.

If you built your Signature Offer for your ideal customer (who's now sitting in front of you), then the program should sell itself.

You should be able to connect the dots of the prospects' pain points and the solutions found in your program.

⇒ You mentioned you wanted to lose 40 pounds by summer. Our clients are losing 1-2 lbs per week on average so you will be right on track to drop that weight before your vacation.

⇒ You mentioned that you struggle with fast-food choices, we have a full guide with exact menu items for you to choose from that are in-line with your goals

⇒ You mentioned when you go to the gym, you don't know what to do. Our Coaches design every workout to tone your entire body so you maximize your time in the gym.

Make The Sale

Now it's time to ask for the sale. This is where most sales are lost. Too many Gym Owners are simply not asking for the sale. Gym Owners often use soft language like, "Just let me know when you are ready to get started."

Soft language puts the ball in the prospect's court, and most people will procrastinate and push the decision down the road. That sets you up for more follow up and admin work. YUCK!

Instead, use phrases like "Let's get you the results you deserve. Do you want to pay-in-full and save 10% or put it on a payment plan?"

Or you could say "Lets get you started Monday. Do you want option A or option B?"

Both of those examples are using "the assumed sale" which is where you assume they are getting started and guiding them into the next step. That's the way to close more deals and avoid further follow up!

BONUS TIP: The Sales Environment

This next section is critical because it's literally the environment they are walking into. The physical objects and the feeling they get from the team are big contributors toward a buying decision.

In any sales situation there are tangibles and intangibles involved. Tangibles are things you can touch, like your certifications on the wall, transformation photos, the agreements, the supplements on the desk, the comfort of the chair, the Inbody machine that gives you a metabolic read out.

They are physical tools to help you achieve a sale, if used properly. They are also looking at your workout space and entry on the way to the sale office. What are they going to see?

The person is judging you whether you know it or not. If the front of the house (gym) is messy, then your prospect is worried your back end (systems) are messy too.
Now they will have more trust issues when giving you their credit card. You've probably had clients who had fears in the back of their mind because they were double drafted by another gym. Don't be that gym yourself!

How you do anything is how you do everything.

One of the biggest issues that plagues the fitness industry is messy, dirty, unorganized gyms that try to charge high ticket rates.

There's a reason customers accept sticky floors at McDonalds, they know they are in the land of the dollar menu.

But they expect spotless white tablecloths and exceptional customer service at Mastro's Steakhouse because of the premium prices.

Are you promising a Mastro's experience but have the cleanliness standards of McDonalds?

Is your fitness equipment always broken like their ice-cream machine?

Is this a clean environment to train or a PlayPlace with mystery skid marks in the ball pit?

People judge how you look and how your space looks from the moment they walk in. It either shows attention to detail or it doesn't. I've walked into many million dollar gyms and from the moment I enter, I can tell why it's achieved that level of success.

Equipment is on storage racks. Wires are hidden, Paint is often refreshed. Desks are clutter free. Everything has a place. The team is dressed professionally. These are the high standards you must have to become a million dollar gym.

Now let's look at the intangibles. These are subtle things but they have a huge influence on the prospect and outcome of the sale. These are things you can't touch, but you know that they are there.

It's when a salesperson is punctual and on-time, has positive energy, a relaxed body language, a voice tone that is warm and upbeat, a confidence in how they carry themselves, and, of course, a conviction in their product and service.

In selling, how you say something is much more powerful than what you say.

If I take the same sentence and say it in a monotone voice or an upbeat voice, it will change how the person feels. Sales is a transference of feelings. And the intangibles are how you say the words in your sales presentation. It's your facial expressions, posture, hand gestures and eye contact.

Both the tangible and intangible aspects contribute to a sale and should be carefully crafted, from start to finish, to result in the highest closing percentage.

If you have questions about this topic, jump into my free Facebook group for Gym Owners.

It's filled with positive, successful and supportive peers who share their best advice , and want to see you win.

Join the group at…

facebook.com/groups/gymreinforcements

Value Bomb 💣

C.H.A.R.M review

- Are you putting your prospects at ease from the start?
- Are you bringing "friend energy" or "buy my stuff energy"?
- Are you building 5x the value before you pitch pricing?
- Are you using soft language or asking for the sale?
- Evaluate your tangibles and intangibles. What are you doing well? What needs improvement?

Chapter 9

Creating The Next Hill

The COVID-19 global pandemic in 2020 was an extremely difficult time for the fitness industry. If you had a gym, then you will never forget it because of the fear that was widespread.

It was crazy to see the government allow the opening of restaurants so people can put forks in their mouths, but were saying that dumbbells were super spreaders.

In our business, I watched our EFT plummet by thousands of dollars every week. Revenue got cut by as much as 65% per location. I made a commitment to not make our team feel the sting. We kept everyone employed and paid their full wages, even though we had 1/3 the clients.

It put us in debt, but I was willing to eat that to keep our team supported. They are always there for me and our clients, I wanted to be there for them when they needed it most.

We did what most Gym Owners did during this time and started offering online workouts, nutrition coaching and planned virtual hangouts, in order to give everyone some positive energy during dark times.

On the bright side, I saw it as a clean slate. Our business was at a full stop, and it was a great time to re-imagine it. I asked myself what I would do differently if I could go back to the beginning. I didn't have a crystal ball, but something told me the days of having boot camps with 50+ people were going to disappear for a while. I thought back to my roots where I did Small Group Training in my garage.

I had been a Fitness Director at a retirement community in the mornings, then I would go home and run Small Group Personal Training sessions in my garage at night. I would have 4-6 people in each session, and it was a tight knit group. I had found most of those clients organically from referrals and by advertising on Craigslist and FB groups. No marketing budget, no ad spend. Just hustle.

It was some of my fondest times as a Coach because I felt the most connected to my clients. Everyone was getting results. I can still remember everyone's' name. And there was some grit to training in my garage. The clients were sweating their face off in the summer and could see their breath when they exhaled in the winter. It was tough but I created a fun experience.

Small Group Training was the spark that lit the fire inside me. It was my original offer to the marketplace. And my team was made of smart Personal Trainers who would often express their desire to demonstrate their skills in a more personalized way to our clients.

It was time to get back to my roots.

I took the "time out" that was COVID to change things up in my business. But you don't have to wait for a global pandemic.

You can change your business at any time.
You're not handcuffed by our past decisions.

I decided I wanted to continue offering boot camp, but we would add on higher ticket services so we could work with fewer people who were paying more. That allowed us to service them better, and hit our revenue goal without needing high volume.

That's when we built our "next hill" for the client in the form of Small Group Training.

The concept of the "next hill' is simple - disengaged clients cancel, engaged clients stay, pay and refer. Your job is to constantly create new hills for your clients.

They need to be challenged. They need something to work toward. The antidote to constantly losing clients is keeping them engaged with an active goal.

It could be a personal goal they are striving for, an interval event or member challenge that you've created. That gives them the what, when and why behind their training.

The most valuable version of a "next hill" for the customer and the company is in the form of services.

You can decide if you want your business to have two hills, three hills, four hills or more. It comes down to the size of your team, the type of services you want to offer and what the marketplace is buying.

Most gyms with a lean team (3 or less people) should offer 1-2 services max. You want to create the core offer that most people join and the next hill for them to ascend to.

Here's an example of what your hills can look like....

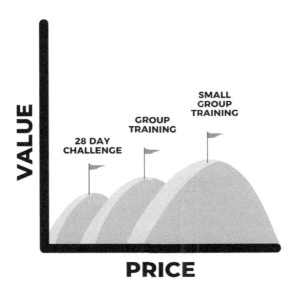

I know that many Gym Owners struggle with the idea of raising their rates on their members. Trust me, I get it. It can make you feel like you're a greedy person.

But you must charge fair market value to stay in business.

That means you must have profits. Without profits you shut your doors which is worse than charging more.

That's why I want to invite you to raise your rates in an ethical way - by adding value.

When you create a new path for your members, that is more valuable than their current service, you'd be surprised how many are willing to step up and pay more. This is especially true for tenured gyms that have been open for years and they are seeing people drop out due to a plateau in results or a desire for more variety.

Once a member has trained with you for a while, they probably start feeling like it's too easy. They've mentally planted a flag in your workouts and check it off as "conquered".

That's why you have to create the next hill for them to conquer.

The other great thing about creating the next hill for your clients is that it costs zero dollars to market it. You just need to offer an invitation to give your existing members a taste.

There's a huge pile of money waiting to be collected within your business, and you are missing out on it by not offering the "next hill" to your clients.

Your foundation program is great but you need the advanced programs for people who want more attention and personalization.
And I don't want you to falsely believe Small Group Training is the only version of a next hill.

Here's some ideas that might be a better fit for you...

- 1-on-1 Personal Training
- Nutrition Coaching
- Mindset Coaching
- Life Coaching
- Online Coaching

Think back to the Signature Offer chapter. This is the next step after they go through that program. This is the higher priced program that 20-50% of your clients will be enrolled in, but it should be more exclusive, solve more problems and give more access to their Coach.

Think of your favorite band. They have general admission, floor seats, front row, backstage pass and VIP experience. All of these are going to be offered for the same show, but they all give the customer a different experience at different budget levels.

Have you only been selling general admission tickets? Time to create your VIP experience.

Value Bomb 💣

Creating / Upgrading Your Clients Next Hill
- What is another service you can offer your clients?
  - *Ex #1: Offer Small Group to Large Group clients*
  - *Ex #2: Offer Nutrition Coaching to Training Only Clients*
- Does your ideal customer want that service? Have you received requests for that service?
- What would you charge so you can make more without working more or adding very few additional hours?
- How can you launch the next hill in the next 30-45 days to your current clients?

Chapter 10

97% Retention All Year Long

I was at a Gym Owner mastermind meeting and the Business Coach asked "what's your monthly retention?". I said "I don't know." The look of disappointment on his face was the gut punch I needed. I knew at that moment that I needed to stop running from my numbers and turn around and face them, head on.

Numbers are cold, hard facts about your business.

There's no emotions or feelings leading you astray. It's just the raw truth. I'm a very optimistic person so I tend to lean toward "things are going great," but looking at my numbers gives me the reality check I need to face the problems in the business.

As I've opened multiple locations, the biggest punch in the gut that I've worked through, many times, is retention. There's nothing more frustrating than investing money in marketing, sales and fulfillment only to have clients cancelling at the same rate. It leaves your business treading water in the same place.

There are two doors to every gym.

Marketing and sales is inviting people to come through the front door. But if the Coaches aren't locking the back door (figuratively, not literally) with good service, then it can create immense frustration.

Solving your retention problem is how you get to massive growth in your business. If you can become a sticky blackhole that just grows and grows and grows…you will become unstoppable and wealthy in the process.

The industry average is 10% attrition (how many people you lose) or 90% retention (how many people you keep). I tend to speak more in retention vs attrition, since I like to focus on the positive.

I now average 97% retention, but it hasn't always been that way. In fact, I vividly remember three of my worst months of retention.

- The month we switched CRMs we lost 12% of our members because we needed to manually collect all of our members credit cards.
- The month we lost 15% of our members because a popular trainer left.
- The month we lost 65% of our members because of COVID.

I've been through some tough times, but I'm here to tell you that it can be fixed if you give focused attention. I know that I've brought up multiple subjects in your business that need focus, but that's where your numbers come in. You need to see which one is the flashing red light that needs that most attention.

If you go back to the Core 10 Metrics and your retention is weak (under 95%) then that's where you should invest your resources, energy, time and attention.

Once you give it focus, it will improve and you can move on to the next constraint. I know it can be tough to hear that problems never go away in your business. But the goal isn't to repeat the same problems over and over. The goal is to evolve your problems and have bigger and better problems over time.

If retention is the area that needs the most attention (which is the case for most fitness businesses) then I want to share 4 tools you can use to fix your retention ASAP.

Retention Tool #1) Member Challenges & Events

I made the mistake of only offering a member challenge 2-3 times per year. To be honest, it was me. I felt weird asking for more money from the people who are already paying me.

I felt like I should be happy with the fact they have a recurring membership and just focus on finding more members.

But the truth is that if a customer loves a company, they want to keep buying stuff from that same company. The same applies to your company, but Gym Owners often fail to present offers to their existing customers to solve more of their problems.

Your core membership solves some problems, but there's probably other problems that stem from it.

One of the problems that's most profitable for you to solve is to give them micro-challenges within the calendar year, where they get a higher level of service for a short period of time.

We call them Member Challenges and they are heavily discounted compared to what the public pays for them, but it gets the members to dial in their nutrition and training to the highest level.

Remember, the more you pay, the more you pay attention.

We plan a Member Challenges or Member Events every month. It could be a members only fitness competition (our version of the CrossFit Games) or a group of members doing a mud run together or a ladies night out party.

All of these events require a paid ticket which is another way to monetize your members and keep them engaged. It serves as a gathering too, which builds bonds and friendships.

One thing to note is that the people who leave tend to be the most isolated. They don't engage with the other members or trainers.

Notice the people who train with you for years and are the most engaged with you, the team and the other clients. One of your top priorities is to get new clients engaged with other folks in your community as quickly as possible.

Make introductions, partner them up with an experienced client for their first 2 weeks, plan gatherings and personally invite new clients.

Create a 12-Month Member Challenge and Event Calendar with an opportunity to sell something to your members. It will help with retention and add to total revenue.

Retention Tool #2) Focused Feedback

We've done mass feedback and focused feedback, let me explain the difference. Mass feedback is when we mass text or email a form to all members. Usually, you tend to get short, vague answers. Focused feedback is when you interview someone 1-1 and really pull the most details from the person. This works much better and it makes the client feel valued and important.

I recommend you do two heavy feedback sessions per year with your current clients and your past clients. Hand pick 3-5 people that can offer valid opinions and who's input you trust. Sometimes you have blinders to what your clients see clear as day.

Here's some great questions to ask...

Current Clients Feedback

1. *What do you like best about our workouts? How can we improve them?*
2. *Who is the main Coach you work with?*
3. *What does your Coach do well? What can they improve on?*
4. *On a scale of 1-10, rate your results. Why?*
5. *On a scale of 1-10, rate our facility cleanliness. Why?*
6. *Do you believe you are getting enough nutrition coaching? Please explain.*
7. *Time to be creative and think big....do you have any bold ideas that we can add to our service to make it better?*

Past Clients Feedback

1. *When you trained with us, what did you like best about our workouts?*
2. *Who was the main Coach you work with?*
3. *What did that Coach do well? What could have been done better?*
4. *On a scale of 1-10, rate the results you got with our program. Why?*
5. *On a scale of 1-10, rate our facility cleanliness. Why?*
6. *Do you believe you got enough nutrition coaching? Please explain.*

7. What could we have done to keep you as a member?

Retention Tool #3) Team Retention

A tool that's often overlooked, but is a massive contributor to client retention, is team retention. Most people like steadiness and consistency in their service, and if the team is constantly turning over that creates unease and the inability for long-term relationships to be built with the client.

Here are some helpful tips to keep your team for years to come.

Be Consistent

If you want consistency then you have to lead with it. That shows up in your attitude, energy and emotional stability. If the leader is quick to anger, blaming others or emotionally unstable the team will bail fast.

Business can be emotionally taxing.

When things are going bad it can feel like they will be bad forever. When things are going good, it's easy to show up as the optimistic leader. I aim to show up neutral, no matter how things are going in the business because I know both are temporary.

Winning seasons end.

Losing sessions end.

My team can count on me being very consistent. I make it to all meetings. I work the same hours every day. I don't get too emotionally stirred up but I'm human and it happens sometimes. I never make a big decision without sleeping on it. I ask for their input in big decisions.

These are ways they can count on me being consistent, so they never feel like the sky is falling.

Create Structure

Even though most people say they crave freedom, the irony is that you can only find that in structure. Jocko Willink says "Discipline equals freedom". Your team might like the idea of having a loose schedule, but it makes your life very difficult as a business owner.

You need predictability and routine. They need it too. We all do better when we can have a dependable routine and build our lives around it. Team members that need constant changes to their schedule are a pain in the neck and make your business 10x more complicated to operate.

I make a conscious effort to hire people with their schedule pre-planned so they can say "yes" or "no" to that schedule during the interview. If they try to negotiate on the schedule, I pass on them.

I'm very clear on what I want, so it's easy to say no if I can't get it.

I know many Gym Owners with Coaches who have non-structured schedules. That makes you feel like the inmates are running the asylum. You need to create a clear job schedule and shop around the market until you can find someone who can fulfill that role as intended.

Think Of Ways To Pay Them More

This is contrary to how most bosses would look at business. They might be thinking "how can I make as much money as possible from my team?"

But there's an old adage from Zig Ziglar - *you can get everything you want out of life if you help people get what they want.*

Fitness tends to attract driven folks who are growth minded and want to make more income over time. It's in your best interest to think of ways to help them make more money. It will help you to retain them as a team member and reduces the chances they need a second job or side hustle. You want them 100% focused on your clients.

Retention Tool #4) Second Tier of Service

This was covered in the previous chapter (Creating the Next Hill) so I won't go into too much detail. But it's interesting to note that the clients in your most expensive program stay the longest. Most Gym Owners falsely believe the opposite. They think that the client will only upgrade for a short period of time.

That's often a self-limiting belief because the Gym Owner or Coach is shopping with their own wallet. They think to themselves "I would never pay that much," but you are not your customer. You know how to train, what to eat and can stay motivated. That's why you are great at helping people who aren't good in that area.

High quality Personal Trainers can retain their clients for years, even though they are charging top tier prices. That's because of the high level of attention, personalization and the deep relationship that's built in that environment.

It sounds counter-productive to offer something more expensive when people are leaving but, trust me, it works.

People are leaving because they need that next hill to conquer. Add a high ticket offer and watch your retention improve drastically.

Value Bomb 💣

Rate Your Retention

- What was your retention % last month?

  (Easy way to get that number - get a list of EFT clients on the 1st of last month and cross check it with the members who were still on EFT the 31st of that same month. Divide those numbers into each other ==> 163 / 170 = 95% retention)

- On a scale 1-10, rate your retention percentage

- When was your last members event or challenge?

  (If more than 60 days, plan something ASAP)

- When was your last feedback collection?

  (If more than 90 days, send out the questions above ASAP)

- Do you offer a second tier of service to your clients? Why or why not?

SECTION III

ASSEMBLE YOUR DREAM TEAM

Chapter 11

Lead The Way

One day I was leaving my gym and it happened to be the end of the session when all the clients huddled together. The Coach and clients stand in a circle, put one hand in the middle and yell an empowering phrase. On this day I heard 30+ clients all yell together the phrase, "Lead the way!" I thought it was really cool because leadership is one of my favorite topics.

One year later, we would be rebranding our gyms, and we had a few concepts in mind. My team and I voted, and the brand that won by a landslide was Lead The Way Fitness.

It really seemed to capture what we wanted to be as a brand. We wanted to develop leaders on our team. We wanted to help our clients become better leaders so they could impact their families. We wanted to be leaders in the community who were involved in local events and charities.

We wanted to be leaders in a fitness industry that was innovative, testing new things and pushing the boundaries.

John Maxwell famously states that *"leadership is influence - nothing less, nothing more."*

And one of the best ways to influence people is to accomplish something great so that people are drawn to you. They naturally ask "How did you do that?" and then you can mentor them to do the same.

Pull energy is far more powerful than push energy.

And the first big pull energy in a company begins with the owner. You are pulling in the clients and the team members based on your character and skills.

I often challenge leaders to ask themselves a tough question: "Are you a leader worth following?" The better leader you become the better talent you will attract. High performers are interviewing you as much as you are interviewing them.

And you must constantly earn their followership by showing up for them every day.

High team member turnover in a gym is often a symptom of poor leadership. Things are not clear. Team members don't feel that there is upward advancement in the company, and they don't feel that their leader cares about them.

I know that, in the past, I've lost great team members due to not being the leader they deserved at that time.

Just like anything, it's a learnable skill, with levels that you can ascend to over time through repetition, learning lessons and experience.

Sharing my leadership lessons in just one chapter will be tough, but my goal is to give you the highest impact items that will create the biggest change in your business. These are my rapid fire leadership lessons.

Lead From the Front

You are the example that's being followed. I only ask my team to do something I've done myself. I've cleaned every square inch of the gym, I've coached the sessions, I've sold the membership, I've had the hard talks. There's nothing I ask them to do that I don't have experience doing.

That's leading from the front.

You gain major brownie points if you show them that you've been in the trenches where they are and that you are willing to jump in there with them. Your team will pay attention to what you do far more than what you say.

I recently learned that we only remember 10% of what was said to us. Think about that for a moment. What was the last video you saw on social media and what did they say exactly? You have probably forgotten.

You must be prepared to deliver repetition if you want to be a great leader. Leading from the front means you also carry the most conviction around the cause. You must remind your team of the mission, vision and values at every interaction. If you aren't fired up about those topics, why should they be?

Hot Potato Problems

When a team member brings a problem to a leader, their main goal should be to empower the person to solve the problem themselves. They threw the potato to you and you must throw it right back. That's hot potato leadership.

Not because you are being lazy and trying to avoid problems, but because you need to develop leaders who can be contributors. If you have 5 or 10 problem solvers vs one, you will go further and you will go faster.

They might say "How should I fix this?" and you can reply "I don't know, what do you think?"

You can Coach them in the right direction if they have no idea, or give them feedback on whatever solutions they present. But both options stimulate them to feel empowered.

If you solve all your team problems on your own then you are training them to be robots that come to you for everything instead of becoming competent individuals who can problem solve on their own. Don't hold on to the hot potatoes or you'll get burned.

One Problem = Two Solutions

We want our team to come to us with problems, frustrations and inefficiencies so we can work on improving it.

My definition of complaining is talking about something to somebody who has no power to fix it. When you talk about a problem, the first step is to talk to the right person who can fix it.

The second step is to always bring solutions. Dumping a problem in someone's lap is being lazy. Everyone needs to help out and be part of the solution.

That's why I've learned to train our team members to always bring two solutions for every problem they share. If someone shares a problem then you can reply with *"Thank you for sharing that. It's important for me to know about our problems. What are some potential solutions we can consider?"*

That quickly teaches everyone to bring their problems and their solutions. As business owners, we get joy from solving problems. That's what draws us to owning a business.

We see a problem and think we can do a better job of solving it. But that will quickly drain you if you try to solve all the problems in the business. You need help. There's no getting around it.

That's how to build your team to be leaders.

Duplicate Your A-Players

If you have a superstar coach or sales person, then you want to pair up your new hires with those folks to duplicate them. That's how a leader creates more leaders.

Most of what needs to be done in a business will be caught, not taught.

People are very good at copying what they see someone else doing. That's why things can go viral on social media. You can see others do a challenge or dance and copy it quickly.

Make sure you have the right person that you want duplicated. I've made the mistake in the past of putting a new hire with a team member who didn't have the best habits, and that got copied into the new person. They shared all their shortcuts on how to do the tasks incorrectly.

Talk about a "slap your head moment."

If you don't have an A-Player to duplicate, then you will need to train them. Training new hires is a fresh start. It's a chance to improve upon the last person who sat in the role.

I don't like staff turnover, but if we lose someone, it's a chance to find an improved version of the last person in that role so we can continue to level up.

Avoid rushing the training and giving it half-effort. You wouldn't do that with a new client. Give your team the same customer service you give your clients. They are the face of your company.

Right Person, Right Seat, Right Bus

Leaders often hire people like themselves, but that causes operational deficiencies because everyone has the same strengths. You want to become hyper-aware of your strengths and your shortcomings. Everyone has them, so embrace them and look for teammates that will fill in your gaps.

Your kryptonite is someone else's superpowers.

For most Gym Owners (I'm generalizing here) they need more help with operations and sales. It's hard to train and lead a salesperson if you personally don't enjoy sales or don't have a strong sales process.

Most people can't lead others where they haven't been before.

That's why I created Gym Reinforcements. To take 100% of lead follow up and sales of the plate of a Gym Owner.

You want the right person in the right seat on the right bus.

The Person= Values, Skills and Character Traits

The Seat = Job Position

The Bus = The Company

Here's a few ways to tell if they are the right person.

1. **DISC Profile Test** - This is immensely powerful to help you see if their personality profile aligns with the role.

- High D - great fit for Manager, Coach or Sales Person (very driven and results focus)

- High I - great fit for Coach or Sales Person (very outgoing and influential)

- High S - great fit for Front Desk, Customer Service role (very calm and patient)

- High C - great fit for Admin or Operations Manager (very analytical and introverted)

Ask the candidate to take a free DISC test to see if it matches the personality of the role they are applying for. This is your first batch of clues they are the right person for the position.

2. References - Most employers do not call references and that's a huge mistake. You get to talk to the person who was in the same position as you and get their feedback on the candidate.

Obviously people will always paint themselves in the best light during an interview. You want to get both sides of the story. This is another place to find more data to drive your decision.

3. Word Association - Ask the candidate to give you 3 words that previous co-workers would use to describe them. This is your chance to see if those words don't match the role or if they are the words their co-workers would really use since you just called them.

The right seat is about matching their values, skills and character traits to a role that will allow their natural gifts to shine.

A person applying for a Coach role wants to be out on the floor, engaging with people and educating their clients, they do not want to be behind a desk. Giving them office work is the fastest way to kill their passion.

The right bus means they are going to work at the right company. It's not fun to deny candidates from getting a position, but here's some food for thought that helped me - just because they aren't a good fit for **my company** doesn't mean they aren't a good fit for **every company.**

They have values, skills and character traits that align with another company out there.

When you pass on a candidate that isn't a good fit, you are helping them to move closer to their ideal company. Keeping people on your team that aren't a good fit is holding them hostage from a company where they will flourish.

Lead From the Back

This type of leadership is something leaders must learn to do as their team builds more competency and confidence in the role. You must step back and have a zoomed out perspective on what is going on in the business.

This is when you step into becoming a true business owner.

A great lesson I learned from leadership expert Jocko Willink was about the difference between a leader **doing** and **leading**.

The military example he shared was if a squad of Marines were under attack, the Squad Leader should not be on the firing line looking through his scope for enemies. That would give him tunnel vision and cloud his ability to see the entire battlefield.

Instead, the Squad Leader needs to step back from the firing line and lead his team. He needs to give them orders and look for opportunities for them to cover and move to a higher position so they can outflank and destroy their enemy.

If he is doing (aiming and firing), then he's not leading (looking for opportunities to win) so his team can be successful in the mission.

Leading from the back means you have to allow your team to do the majority of the "doing" so you can focus on the "leading". That doesn't mean you're better than them or above them. It's a different part of work. It's the most challenging work. It requires making big decisions, taking calculated risks, taking full responsibility if it doesn't go well and analyzing the data.

It means looking at your business from a zoomed out perspective and figuring out what needs attention. Which metrics are going well and which ones need improvement. What is a critical project that needs to be completed and what can go in the "parking lot" of ideas.

Too many Gym Owners are busy doing things but aren't leading their teams. This was a tough pill for me to swallow because this was me for years. I enjoy doing. If a certain area needed help I wanted to be the hero to come to the rescue. But that can only get you so far.

You can only muscle your way to a certain point of growth.

At some point, you have to stop focusing on your hustle muscle and start building your leadership muscle.

Final Thoughts

Leadership is a moving target. That's why you must constantly grow in this area. I've made some great progress in this area, but I certainly have more to learn. This can be the "unsexy" side of business.

Most Gym Owners want to chase the rush and excitement of getting new leads and sales. But leadership is the long term investment in your business that creates more stability and a stronger foundation for your business.

I opened too many gyms too quickly (6 gyms in 6 years), and it came crashing down because I didn't have the leadership foundation in place to support it. I knew the basics - sign a lease, buy equipment, find awesome Coaches to run sessions. I thought I could do that and move to the next town to rinse and repeat.

But I was missing a leader and it fell apart quickly because of that. You can have awesome systems but if there's no leader driving culture and maintaining standards it can all fall apart. Be the leader your team deserves today and start building the leaders you need for tomorrow.

I don't want to sugar coat it. It will be harder than you thought. It will take longer than you thought. It will cost more than you thought. But the good news is that it will pay off bigger than you could have ever dreamed.

Value Bomb 💣

Leadership Development Questions

- Which of these leadership lesson do you need to implement?
- Who is a leader on your team that you're currently developing? Set a deadline date to give them more responsibility.
- What do you need to get off your plate next?
- Who is the next leader you will need to develop?

Chapter 12

If They're Not Gold, We Hold

Yes, I will wake up everyday at 330am." I couldn t believe this Coach that was applying for the job was willing to ride their bike almost 20 miles one way to open the gym.

But something told me he was good for it. The man standing in front of me was Sal Chavez. He was looking me dead in the eye and he was oozing confidence. I decided to take the chance and go for it.

I consider myself a strong people reader and my gut was telling me that Sal was what we needed on the team. But there were some obvious red flags. He didn t have a car and his license was suspended due to some bad decisions in his past. And he would have to wake up at 330am to ride his bike from Pasadena to Monrovia to open the gym on time.

But my gut told me to take the risk. I liked that he was so hungry. I enjoyed working with former military and he was a Marine Corpsman who was deployed in the middle east.

After the military, he spent a short time in the medical field before deciding to leave because he didn t agree with the pill-pushing culture. He wanted to be on the preventive side of the fight.

I decided to take the leap and give Sal a chance. Today, he s the General Manager of 3 locations and my trusted partner in our brick-and-mortar business. He s a remarkable leader and I never would have had him on the team if I followed a rigid hiring process.

But that was definitely an exception. In fact, I've made more bad hiring choices by operating from my gut. This is a lesson I want to pass on to you my dear reader so you don't have to repeat it.

If you are a Gym Owner then I'm assuming you're like me - very optimistic. You can see the good in people and why it will all work out. You need to be balanced out by someone who doesn't look at the glass half full.

As an optimistic person, it's easy for me to see the good in people and their huge potential. I've hired team members off a "good feeling" and it bit me in the butt. I've dealt with stolen cash, people quitting on day one, Coaches no showing their shifts and coaches actively prospecting clients during our sessions. You know, those fun business owner problems that only business owners can relate to.

Creating a hiring process is good for everyone - the business owner, the candidate, the company and the team. When things are rushed, its a negative experience for all.

One of the best things you can do as a leader is to package your standards in short phrases that convey a framework or process into memorable one-liners.

One-liners speed up communication and decision making because we are all on the same page and use the same vocabulary.

The one-liner we use when hiring is **if they're not gold, we hold.**

I've hired out of desperation and every single time I regret it. I know that we want the relief of having a team member owning a part of the business but it's not worth it if you are going to have find a replacement for them sooner after.

We only want gold on our team and we cannot be the gold standard of fitness if we allow silver and bronze onboard.

After you set the standard (we only want gold) you have to clearly identify what that looks like so the team can spot it and tell you if the candidate is a good fit or not.

I've also learned that you get what you pay for as an employer. If you've ever run a low price trial offer, then you probably got lower quality leads that couldn't afford your ongoing membership.

The same goes for your team.

Treat your team like gold and they will treat your clients like gold.

If you pay super low wages, you will get applicants with little to no experience. They might be a 5 out of 10 and now you need to close a big gap of skills.

This might be what you need to do if you're on a budget and you have the time to invest in team development. That's where I started, but I loved teaching and pouring into my team every day. Not everyone enjoys training new hires.

If you pay more, you might get a 8 out of 10 that requires very little training and will be a plug-and-play team member.

I say "might" because it's not guaranteed you will find a strong candidate just because you're paying more, but the chances are higher.

If you pay well you want to find someone that comes with skills, factory installed.

Once you find the gold, here's 3 steps of interviewing....

Step #1) The 15-Minute Get-To-Know-You

The 15-Minute Get-To-Know You should be done over the phone or Zoom to save you time. You want to have your questions prepared in advance to make sure the candidate fits your values, doesn't have scheduling conflicts and understands the details of the role clearly.

I've seen many applicants who were fast to apply and didn't take the time to read the role details, so make sure they have a full understanding of what they are signing up.

It's a great time to share the #1 priority of the role, the KPI and how you expect them to achieve both. You can often catch a bad fit just by asking very basic questions at this stage of the hiring process. This is your first layer of screening.

On this call you want to screen their character and check their self-awareness.

Here's a few things to look out for....

- *Do you sense an unhealthy ego?*
- *Are they using more "I" statements than "we" statements?*
- *Are they more driven by the paycheck or passion?*
- *How do they talk about past employers? Positive or negative light?*
- *What's their main motivation to work hard?*
- *How do they snap themselves out of a funk?*
- *What is the last failure they had and what did they learn from it?*
- *Can they admit to their strengths and weaknesses? (Someone once told me they had no weaknesses. Needless to say, they didn't get hired.)*

I'm also screening for anything on their resume that doesn't match the story they are telling me.

I had someone apply once that mentioned they worked for a company for 6 months but when we did a reference check (yes, you should do them), they were at that previous job for 3 weeks.

I also like to do rapid-fire questions where I ask the candidate to rate themselves on a 1-10 for specific skills that apply to the job role.

Things like…
- Programming
- Form Correction (Verbal)
- Form Correction (Hands On)
- Nutrition Coaching
- Communication
- Tech Savvy
- Remembering First Names
- Sales
- Motivation

If they seem to have the right values, skills and character traits, we push them forward to the next step.

Step #2) Skills and Aptitude Test

The second step (Skills and Aptitude Test) is about putting them into the role for a real life look at them doing the primary activity.

For a Coach, that means having them run 1-2 sessions and if it's a salesperson, we will give them our sales script, let them study it for a day, then do a couple role play calls with team members. I want the team's feedback because they will be working with this person too!

Aptitude means it's a natural ability, so you should see their skills shine through. It's a great way to see if they sink-or-swim with no training.

Companies like Chik-Fil-A have their training dialed in to the point where they can take teenagers with no work experience and give them world-class, customer-service training. They have a big budget and decades of experience on how to get someone from 0-10.

You are likely a small business owner and don't have the same budget, time or experience as them. That's why you need to find someone who is ready to go and needs some slight polishing to fit your business model.

Step #3) Team Acid Test

The last step is the Team Acid Test and that's where we do a group interview and allow everyone on the team to ask questions.

One of my favorite steps is when we do a Stress Response exercise.

We have a batch of questions where we lay out scenarios that could happen or have happened in the past and we ask how they would handle it.

Here's a few we use...

- A client is feeling frustrated because they aren't seeing results. How do you handle that?
- You have to run the 5:30am session, what time would you show up to prepare?
- You are informed the toilet is clogged, how do you respond?
- You are mid-session and a client looks dizzy or lightheaded, what would you do?
- The power abruptly goes out. No music. No lights. What would you do in that situation?
- A prospect walks in during the middle of a session asking for information about our program and you're the only team member available, what would you do?

We are screening for thinking on their feet, problem solving and resilience during difficult situations. We are a fast moving team and we need to see if they can keep up with the pack. That's something we value on our team.

You may have different values, so craft your hiring steps for what's right for you.

During this team interview we want to see if they can vibe with our team. Do they feel like one of us? Can they keep up with our banter? Do they feel comfortable being part of the conversation?

I know that I bring my views and opinions, but it's helpful to hear my team's observations too. Sometimes they catch things I miss or interpret answers differently and it's helped us to dodge bullets in the past.

I recommend always getting two other people's opinions before making a hire. It will save you a lot of time, energy and money.

Fire Fast, Hire Slow

The rubber meets the road in the first 30 days, and you should closely observe production. If we don't see meaningful production then we have to part ways quickly.

Something to consider when you are running a small business with a crew of 2-5 people - every individual makes up a big percentage of your workforce.

If you have 4 team members then each person is 25% of your team!

That means each person has to bring value to the business and produce, otherwise they can't stay.

At first you coach them up and then you coach them out.

If they are not meeting their KPIs, it's much easier to explain to the person why they cannot stay on the team. Numbers are cold hard facts. It's not an attack on them as a person.

It's 100% based on performance. That's why it's so important each role has a measurable KPI.

Keep Your Standards High and Squats Low

After someone joins your team, the standards set the pace. They are the minimum effort allowed. That's why you want to maintain high standards with your team.

As James Clear stated in his book *Atomic Habits*...

we don't rise to our goals, we fall to our standards.

Team members that are like a rock will weigh you down. They drag down the team. They always have problems and no solutions. They do the minimum to remain employed.

On the other hand, rock stars have their own set of standards that they bring to a company. If you don't maintain high standards, they will leave. They bring solutions and want to see everyone one win.

You want a team of rock stars, not rocks.

When you have rock stars in place, you can accomplish 10x more then you ever could alone. And people are fluid. They change. Sometimes they can start as a rock star and go through life changes that transform them into a rock. And it can go the other way too. Navigating those changes is part of being a leader!

Here's a side-by-side snapshot...

Rocks 🪨	Rock Stars 🤘
Require Pushing	*Push You*
Don't Fulfill Their Needs and Force You To Do Aspects of Their Job	*Fulfill Your Needs By Succeeding In Their Role*
Don't Know What You Want and Aren't Looking for the Answer	*Know What They Want, What It Looks Like and How To Achieve It*
Don't Associate with Rockstars and Repel Rockstars	*Demand To Only Work with Rockstars*
Cause Problems	*Find Solutions*
Don't Understand Why Your Bar Is Set So High	*Continually Look For Ways to Raise The Bar*
Do The Bare Minimum To Remain on the Team	*Looks for Ways to Overachieve and Earn More Of Your Trust / Business*

Value Bomb 💣

Review Your Hiring Process

- Do you need to implement the Get-To-Know-You Call?
- Do you need to implement the Skills and Aptitude Test?
- Do you need to implement the Team Acid Test?
- How many people are on your team?
  (Divide total team members into 100 to calculate their total influence on your team. EX: 100/5 = 20%)
- Do you have any rocks weighing you down?
- Who are your rockstars that you want to duplicate?

Chapter 13

Tools for High Performing Teams

I have a quarterly performance review with my Coaches where we look at what they are doing well, set goals for the future, and learn what struggles they're encountering in their role. I look forward to these meetings because it's a chance to stop our day-to-day grind and ask great questions that help us improve.

At one of the meetings, I vividly remember a Coach saying *"Dustin, I just want to win and I can't tell if I'm doing a good job or not. I need a clear and simple way to track winning."*

At that moment, I knew I was failing as a leader. We didn't have a clear way to see if we were a winning team or a losing team. But it was freeing to hear from my team they want to be led. That was the permission I needed to change things for the better.

High performers have high expectations. They want to be led. They want accountability. They want to see the score. They want to compete. They want to win.

Below are some helpful tools I implemented to help my team to start winning at a higher level.

High Performing Tool #1) The Scorecard

You probably heard the phrase "what gets measured gets done." If you are not routinely looking at numbers then your team doesn't believe they are important.

Winners want to clearly see if they are winning, and one of the best ways to measure that is to create a scorecard.

Sports teams measure their success based on their score. It's how you get to championships.

Are we winning? Are we losing? How much time is on the clock? All of those questions can be answered when you look at the score in a sports game.

Each person on the team must own a measurable outcome or KPI. If you cannot measure, it then it's not fair to hold them accountable to it. We must be able to run reports, or find the data we need in our system, so we can enter it weekly into the scorecard.

If the numbers are on track, the team member can keep chugging along and doing their thing.

If the numbers are off track, the team member must own up to it with an action plan to improve it.

Build a simple scorecard for your team to update weekly that includes who is responsible for which numbers, the KPI goal and the KPI that was actually achieved.

Seeing these numbers, week after week, begins to train into your mind patterns. You know what an average, above average and below average week looks like in all areas of your business.

And it's an opportunity for you and the team member to discuss feedback that is 100% performance driven, not an attack on the person.

Sometimes people take feedback personally which is why it's important to start the talk with reminding them that you are looking at numbers and how to improve them. Oftentimes, it can turn into a talk about their personal life but only if they choose to go that direction.

Here's an example Scorecard…

Name	Category	Goal	Week #1	Week #2	Week #3	Week #4
Mike	Leads	25				
Mike	Trials Sold	5				
Mike	Membership Conv %	72%				
Mike	Memberships Sold	3				
Jessica	Drops	0.5				
Jessica	EFT Added	$750				
Jessica	EFT Lost	$150				
Jessica	EFT Net	$600				
Jessica	Total Members	210				
Samantha	Retention %	97%				

High Performing Tool #2) Chain of Command

One of the simple things a leader can do is create a clear chain of command in their company. First you must identify your main departments. Four common departments in a gym are marketing, sales, coaching and operations.

Now you need to create a simple organizational chart that shows the head of those departments (Director of Marketing, Head Coach, etc.) and write in the person's name who owns that seat. It's okay if it's you in all 4 leadership seats, but your goal is to build leaders and hand these seats over to them.

This helps your team to know who does what and who reports to who. We revisit our Org Chart twice a year because it's a great re-alignment of duties and chain of command. And our job roles change, so it's good to keep everyone updated on the newest version.

This provides clarity to your team and it forces you to think through every position a couple times per year.

Below is a sample org chart. The owner is the visionary with the big ideas and innovations who recruits A-players. They might sit in the Director of Marketing seat and coordinate their marketing plans with the Ad Agency they work with, unless they run their own ads internally.

Next is their Team Leader which could also be a Head Coach or Manager. They lead the coaching and sales team members. And finally there should be a leader on the operations side of the house.

They help with financials, bill pay, payroll, keeping the gym stocked up, keeping the cleaners accountable, entering agreements and can also help with customer support. This is an Administrative Assistant, Operations Manager or Facility Director job title.

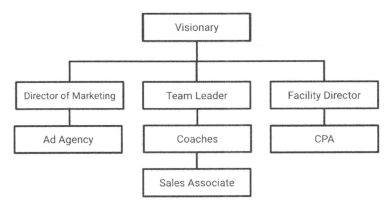

High Performing Tool #3) Weekly Team Meetings

Teams need a structured time when they know they bring up issues, struggles and clarifying questions. As a leader, it can sound counterproductive to ask for problems from your team, but it's the only way to get ahead of issues.

You don't want a teammate to suffer in silence and then blow up on someone out of frustration. Most people don't want to bother you with something "small" or they might say "I know you are busy so I didn't bring it up." That's no way for a high performing team to operate. You have open and honest communication.

And, in the beginning, when they are new they might not want to rock the boat with problems. You must actively pull problems out of their head to show them "we love hearing problems" because that means we get to solve them and make things better. Only dead people have no problems.

There's a phrase I love from Cameron Herold...

no agenda, no attenda

As a leader, come prepared for the meeting with a simple and effective agenda. We use a simple agenda from the EOS Toolbox.

1. Wins - How Are You Winning Personally or Professionally?
2. Headlines - Announcements / Reminders
3. Scorecard - Review Core 10 Metrics

4. Issues - Tackle Problems and Create Action Steps

5. To-Do List - Who's Doing What and What's The Deadline

6. Shout Outs - Team Members Shout Out Another Team Member

We are in and out in 60 minutes. Most meetings feel boring and pointless. Make them fun. Keep everyone on track and avoid tangents. Be respectful of everyone's time and start and end on time. Your team will start to look forward to team meetings, and you will begin to solve big problems together.

High Performing Tool #4) The Gift of Feedback

The fastest growing companies have fast feedback loops. Any app you use today went through countless iterations based on how users responded to it. They have the advantage of getting it real-time from people who download it and interact with it.

In a brick and mortar setting, we must be actively collecting feedback from our clients while giving ourselves and each other constructive criticism as well.

A great quarterly exercise to implement is recording game film. Have each Coach record a full session and post in a group chat or closed FB group for other Coaches to watch and offer feedback.

The Coach should also give themselves feedback first, by sharing what they are doing well and what they can improve. This is no different than a professional athlete watching their game film with their Coach to improve for the next game. Feedback should be timely, often and actionable.

No feedback holds the team back.

They cannot grow without it. If we want to develop our team quicker, then it comes down to how frequently you provide feedback.

VALUE BOMB 💣

Team Tools Implementation

- Do you have a scorecard with KPIs for your team?
- Have you built an org chart? If so, is it updated?
- Do you have a weekly team meeting? If not, when can you start?
- Are you actively giving feedback to team members?

Chapter 14

The Root of All Team Problems

Here's a funny story that involved my wife, MaryBeth, selling household items on Facebook. We go through a spring cleaning twice a year and sell all the random stuff we don't use or things we have no emotional attachment to. MaryBeth decided to sell a rug in our living room and upgrade to a bigger one that would better fit the space.

She took photos and posted them on Facebook Marketplace at a killer price, and since we had a truck, we even offered to deliver the rug. Talk about a grand slam offer! Within minutes she was getting flooded with DMs from interested buyers.

One person stood out among the others because they lived a block away and they were willing to pay the asking price.

This is how the DM conversation went…

Buyer: Hey, I'm very interested. That's a great price. Is it still available?

MaryBeth: Yes, it's still available.

Buyer: Great!! I live on Maple Street. Can you deliver it?

MaryBeth: Yes I can deliver it at 2pm if that works.

Buyer: 2pm is perfect!! See you then. Here's my address.

MaryBeth: See you soon. I know you will enjoy it.

Seems like a normal conversation right? Here's where things changed. The lady came out and said "Where is the couch?"

MaryBeth was confused because they were chatting back and forth about the rug for sale.

Turns out the lady didn't read the title of the post and bought it based on the photos. She saw the couch and rug and assumed that both of them were included for that price. It was a complete miscommunication error because neither of them ever said "rug" in the messages. Go back and read the convo....they kept referring to "it".

These communication mishaps happen every day in business. People on your team learn their communication skills from other people (friends, family, social media) and it's often not clear.

Communication Red Flag #1: Soft Talk
I've seen too many vague team communications like…

- I will reach out to them (To who?)
- We will have to wait and see (For what?)
- I will try to reach out to her (Try in what way?)
- Let me get back to you about that (When exactly?)

The examples above are soft talk and are missing a specific action, deadline and owner of the task. You must have zero tolerance for soft talk in your business. We must know who is doing what and when it's due to be a high performing team.

One trait that all great leaders have in common is their ability to communicate. Authors, public speakers, CEOs, pastors and activists must be able to share their ideas in a simple and easy to understand way. They must be able to translate their vision to others quickly and precisely. The more words they use, the more watered down things get. The vision can get lost in translation.

The root of all team problems is communication.

Heck, I think it's the root cause for most problems that exist in the world - divorces, wars, business failures, politics, social media arguments.

Most people are not communicating effectively, and it causes major problems for everyone in their life.

If a leader cannot explain a task or project clearly, they are going to be far less effective as a leader. We are sending and receiving communication all day, so it's one of the most important skills to master.

One of the most important common places for communication errors is in written format.

That's because when people read a text or email, they might emphasize one word more than another. They might read the word as if it's written in all caps when that wasn't the sender's intent.

Below is an exercise I do with my team to illustrate how written communication is so easy to screw up as a writer and reader.

Read the variations of the sentence and emphasize the words in **CAPS** when you read it…

- **I** didn't say she was beautiful
- I **DIDN'T** say she was beautiful
- I didn't **SAY** she was beautiful
- I didn't say **SHE** was beautiful
- I didn't say she **WAS** beautiful
- I didn't say she was **BEAUTIFUL**

That one sentence can have 6 variations based on what the reader emphasizes in their mind. It's really easy to miscommunicate in written format. That's why I believe more fights happen on social media than in real life.

Facebook would make you believe people are fist-fighting all around town, but you go out and everyone is fine just living their lives. It's a warped reality.

Being a keyboard warrior is easy because you can be a complete jerk with no consequence of ever meeting this person. It's a license to treat the other person like trash, and it's just plain ugly.

When your team is vague or not crystal clear, it hurts the business. Everything must be as simple as possible.

Simplicity scales. Complexity fails.

If you make things simple, they are easy to teach to new hires, they are easy to remember, they are easy to convey to the customer, they are easy to sell and they are easy to hold people accountable.

A great exercise to do with your team is a "simplicity audit". Ask your team members about your systems and their knowledge about how things work. The simpler things are, the easier it will be for them to memorize. The more complicated, the more blank looks you will get.

You could ask…

- How do we get leads?
- How do we convert them?
- What's our signature offer?
- How much is our monthly membership?

- What happens if a client needs to freeze?
- What is our cancellation policy?
- What are the components of a great session?
- If a client needs help with nutrition, what do we offer them?
- How should we greet the clients when they enter the gym?
- What is our dress code?

Asking these questions to your team will give you all the feedback you need on the simplicity of your business model. It will also reveal what needs to be simplified or requires re-training.

Communication Red Flag #2: Lack of Awareness

I mentioned earlier that a DISC test is a great tool to use when hiring talent. It's also powerful to better understand your existing team. Something I learned from the DISC Profile is that each person has a different personality with a different set of filter questions.

- D - Direct, Results Orientated, Firm, Strong Willed, Forceful
  ⇒ **They hear and say WHAT we need to do**

- I - Outgoing, Enthusiastic, Optimistic, High Spirited, Lively
  ⇒ **They hear and say WHO will be involved**

- S- Patient, Humble, Even-Tempered, Steady, Accommodating
  ⇒ **They hear and say HOW we are going to do it**

- C - Analytical, Reserved, Introverted, Precise, Systematic
  ⇒ **They hear and say WHY are we making this change**

You might read that and think to yourself, OMG that's totally me!

I did the same thing. That's why I encourage Gym Owners that you have to learn your teams DISC profile and teach them yours.

When the team knows each other's personality types, they can better understand how they think, which tasks they excel at and how they bring the most value to the team.

A strong team has variety. If a business leader hires duplicates of themselves the business will be redundant and weaker. If it's a mix of strengths it will be much more durable, adaptable and able to adjust to market conditions.

Most business leaders would rank High D which means they know "what" they want done but they tend to skip "how" they want it done or "who" is involved or "why" it must be done.

This can cause team friction.

It's important to speak to all DISC profiles when communicating to your team.

Example of High D communication…
- *Coaches, I want you to ask for referrals each month. This begins immediately. Let's get it done, no excuses.*

Example of DISC communication…
- *Coaches!! I need your help. (WHO) Your goal is to get 2 referrals per month (WHAT) and here's why….when you ask for a referral it helps us achieve our mission of creating 50 transformations by the end of the year. (WHY)*

  Referrals are pre-sold and it makes our members stay longer too when they have friends training with them. Three of the best ways to get referrals are…1) Ask Members after a session….2.) Post an invitation on your social media…..3.) Wear your ABC Boot Camp t-shirt around town. (HOW)

It took me a long time to figure out that not everyone is wired the same as me, and to be an effective leader, I need to speak to all personality types. I was very "what" driven and I would get confused when people would ask for the how, why and who.

"Just figure it out" was my default response.

But that's the lowest level of leadership. We need to bring more clarity to the situation and be prepared for all personality types to be successful.

We got our entire team to complete the DISC profile and it was a game changer for our communication. People who would often butt heads now understood each other better.

We also added it into our interview process and required everyone to take a DISC test to see if their results match the role they are applying for.

If you want to get a custom leadership growth plan for you and your team, I recommend working with Rich Lohman. Learn more about his services at RichLohman.com

We have worked with Rich for months and my team said it's one of the best investments we ever made to enhance team communication and understanding each others personality types so we can work better together.

Communication Red Flag #3: Direct vs Indirect Coaching

I had a Gym Owner buddy reach out to me with frustration. He owned a big box gym and a handful of members were driving him crazy. They would use the squat racks and wouldn't rack their plates.

Most gym junkies know the unwritten rule - **RACK YOUR PLATES!**

No one gave these members the memo. His attempt at fixing the problem is where you can learn a valuable communication lesson.

He shared with me that he did 3 things to get the message across to these members…

1. Hung a sign at the squat racks that they must rack their plates.

2. Sent out a blast email to all members reminding them of the re-rack policy.

3. Got on the speaker system and made an announcement when those members were training in the gym.

But the issue continued. None of those solutions worked for him. Finally I laughed and said "have you tried talking to the person one-on-one?"

He shamefully admitted that he did not try that yet.

I get it, constructive criticism can feel like an attack on the other person. The majority of people do not like confrontation.

They will try 100 indirect and passive-aggressive ways to share their frustration with the other person. But it almost never works. The fastest way to fix your problems is to attack them head on.

Here's my public service announcement - IT'S OK TO BE DIRECT!

You don't have to be mean, rude or a jerk. You can just get straight to the point, have eye contact and tell the person how their actions are negatively affecting others.

People are adults and can handle the feedback and, if they can't, they probably won't be in your world for very long. That's ok.

Trying to fix things indirectly rarely works. In fact, I would like to challenge you for a moment and ask yourself the last time you fixed something by being indirect.

Can't think of an example? That's because it doesn't happen.

Things only get better when we are direct.

- We fix our health when we get direct and confront our eating and exercising habits

- We fix our finances when we get direct and confront our bank statements

- We fix our relationships when we get direct and ask how we can show up better

-

- We fix our business when we get direct and confront our numbers

Most people need to be more direct.

And this applies to giving encouragement too. Most people do not internalize a general compliment or statement. When we say *"Hey Team, you are doing a great job."* No one really feels that is directed toward them.

But when I say *"Hey Shannon, you are doing a great job!"* she immediately feels that direct praise.

Praising others and correcting them is more effective when it's direct.

Value Bomb 💣

Team Tools Implementation

- On a scale of 1-10, rate your team communication
- Have you taken a DISC test? Has your team taken it?
- Do you tend to be more indirect or direct with communication?

Chapter 15

Is This Your Best Work?

You've probably heard of the infamous director Steven Spielberg. He directed *Jaws, Jurassic Park, Indiana Jones, Saving Private Ryan, Minority Report, War of the Worlds, ET, Hook, West Side Story* and countless other blockbuster movies.

Steven Spielberg has been nominated for 19 Academy Awards, has won 3 of them and has a net worth of 4 billion dollars.

Years ago, Spielberg's movie crew was being interviewed by a leadership expert to find out how he was able to get them to create such remarkable films. Every crew member said a version of *"he got more out of me then I knew I had."*

Things aren't easy when you are on set with Spielberg. He demands more out of you. His crew gets stretched and pushed when working with him. Most of the big production movies say he gets **double the results** from the same crew that other Hollywood directors use.

And many of the crew members request to stay on with Spielberg for future projects. That's what allows him to work on two projects at once. He retains his talented staff.

During the interview, the crew members revealed a piece of his leadership magic. They said if you were on set with Spielberg, there's a line you would hear from him over and over again - *is this your best work?*

- *A casting director would say they found the best actors...is this your best work?*

- *A cameraman would say he has the perfect scenic shot...is this your best work?*

- *A set designer would say they are ready for the action scene.....is this your best work?*

- *A costume creator would say they are ready for a fitting....is this your best work?*

He stopped people throughout their day of busy activities and had them quality check themselves. He forced them to think to themselves…

- *"Am I just checking the box to get this done?*
- *"Am I bringing my best so we can win Academy Awards?"*

He wanted to win. He demanded it from his team. He kept the standards high.

Giving 50% is exhausting, giving 100% is exhilarating.

You can do the same in your business. You can win. You can create more impact and income. It all comes down to the actions you take daily. It's easy to get caught up in the small things.

That's why you need to build a lead machine, add sales multipliers and assemble a dream team.

That way your business grows and gets bigger and better every year.

Don't make the same mistake as most people who consume a high amount of books and self-development content. They read a book and add it to the shelf. Read, shelf, repeat. They consume without creating.

Tony Robbins says…

Knowledge isn't power, it's only potential power. The real power is execution.

If you are a Gym Owner, I wrote this book specifically for you.

This book has everything you need to get to the next level. You can build a million dollar fitness business with everything I've given you.

Use the tools, action steps and value bombs outlined in this book to upgrade your current service.

My goal is to help you achieve your goals quicker than me. To have the student become the teacher. To have the reader become the leader.

Look at your business and ask yourself....is this my best work?

If you need any help along the way, please reach out to me. I'm here to serve Gym Owners and help them build the business of their dreams. It's time to get to work!

Dustin Bogle

FB Group: facebook.com/groups/gymreinforcements

Podcast: Lunch with a Punch

Website: GymReinforcements.com
IG: @dustin.bogle

Gym Owner Success Stories

Christina Marie

We joined Gym Reinforcements 2 months ago and from day one I was so pleased to see the team work. The entire team is flexible, and very open to learn our specific gym location procedures. They take action immediately and implement. Being in the gym business industry is a lot of hard work and we needed a team for marketing, sales, and onboarding.

It was hard to find a company that actually does what they say and promise to do. With Dustin he was sharp from day one and easy to work with. Onboarding was easy for myself and his team are very fast, effective learners. So far, we have signed up more people than we ever had on memberships. The success of his program has been incredible so far. I love that we added them to handle the marketing of our business in addition to sales and onboarding.

It's amazing to send over what we want - pics, videos, details and they arrange and put it together for us and implement immediately after. Lastly, I jumped on the monthly marketing call this month only to find out MORE VALUE!!!

Dustin helps you to plan your marketing in advance. He gives you ideas on what to sell externally and internally to your members. This makes business nice in the aspect that we have more ideas and options if we choose to use them. I am excited to see where the next few months take us. Thankful and grateful for Gym Reinforcements!

James Swift

I've known and been trained by Dustin over the years through Fit Body Boot Camp. When I saw he created Gym Reinforcements, I knew I could trust Dustin to help us excel since hiring has been such a challenge in recent months.

The team he has built through Gym Reinforcements has exceeded our expectations. He has built a detail oriented team looking to help gym owners staff themselves with a quality sales and service team so we can work ON our business rather than IN our business.

His team has already returned 1.5X our monthly investment in sales revenue. The 1 year ROI will be 5X+, all the while taking many of our daily/weekly administrative tasks off our plate. It's been incredible! This has been the easiest hire we've made since opening our facility 4 years ago.

Jody Campbell

I have been following Dustin Bogle as a business mentor for years. In that time, I have utilized his advice, motivational tools, business systems and techniques. He has provided me with a wealth of knowledge and, more importantly, a stockpile of tools to grow and sustain my business!

Gym Reinforcements has been the best investment I have made in my business, increasing my sales by 40%. Dustin s willingness to share what he has learned through his vast experience in the fitness industry makes him and his team an invaluable resource! This guy is THE BEST!

Jody Campbell
Owner- Macomb Fit Body Boot Camp

Katy Gomes
We have been using Gym Reinforcements for 1 month now and it has been a game changer for us. Our numbers have nearly doubled since bringing them on board and I can't speak highly enough about them. They are hard working, reliable, trustworthy, and all around a great addition to our team. If you have been on the fence about teaming up with them then you need to stop what you are doing and get in touch with them ASAP!

Jake Duncan
Gym Reinforcements has been a complete saver for my gym business. Not just for gaining new leads and potential clients but with tools and resources for internal member retention as well. The GR team gives a massive support system to make sure you are ready to dominate each month.

They stay in constant communication, giving you updates and reports about new leads. I needed help with follow up in my business badly and they came to the rescue. Doing my own lead follow up was not my strength.

Now it's one of the strongest areas of my business. Once you go "all in" with Gym Reinforcements you don't want to leave. It's just too good NOT to have. I wasn't sure at first. Of course. you have your doubts. But when you start to see the return coming in, you know you made the right decision. I am very appreciative of Gym Reinforcements.

Zach Shagi

Gym Reinforcements is the best! They are extremely detailed, focused people who truly want the best for your fitness business. They go above and beyond what they promise each and every day. We are so thankful we signed up with their program several years ago. We haven t looked back since! Thank you Gym Reinforcements! We look forward to even more success with our partnership for many years to come!

Ian Bowen

Gym Reinforcements has been a great addition to my business. Being a Gym Owner my expertise is in getting my clients results. Selling, lead nurturing and administrative tasks although critical to my business are not in my wheelhouse.

Gym Reinforcements has been a game changer for me. It has freed up my time so I can focus on my greatest areas of impact in my business. Since I hired them I've seen a positive ROI month. My

EFT and total memberships have increased and I ve had more peace of mind with Dustin and the GR team in my corner.

Marcy Kendall

I own Contra Loma Fit Body Boot Camp and I just celebrated 5 years in business. My first few years in business I was pretty much doing it all. Coaching, follow up, sales, accounting, janitorial, you name it, and I was doing it.

Of course during this time, I discovered what I was good at and what I wasn't good at. Sales and follow up were my nemesis so I put that on the back burner and focused on what I was good at. Well it didn't take long for me to see the effects of not focussing on those areas.

I knew that the only way to get more people through my doors and add to my EFT would require me to put sales and follow up at the top of my to do list. Since I already knew that I wasn't the best person to accomplish these tasks, I started looking for help. I trained and hired 4 different "sales managers" and It didn't work out. What I learned is that it takes a special kind of person to do fitness sales.

After another year of failed attempts, I contacted Dustin and begged him for some help. I have now been with Gym Reinforcements and I couldn't be more happy. I have a dedicated Sales Associate who has taken over all of my follow up and sales. I have been able to increase my revenue and gain peace of mind knowing that my leads are not falling through the cracks. By having GR on my team, I am able to focus on what I do best which is coaching and nurturing my members. No, this is not a cheap service, but it is worth every penny. It is one of the best investments I have made for my business.

Jodi Hartel

I LOVE my Gym Reinforcements team. They always go above and beyond in all they do. They are a vital part of the team and without them I d be lost, overworked, overwhelmed, up a creek without a paddle.

Gym Reinforcements has helped me so much to help me with my business and I m so grateful they exist. They have helped us know that our lead follow up is being done by an expert Sales Rep and it helps me sleep at night knowing all of our leads are getting great customer service.

Thank you so much Gym Reinforcements. I wish I had this service before we opened doors!

Toni Lacey

I can t tell you how much Gym Reinforcements has done for me and my business. I honestly hired them on a whim and thought it would be a temporary fix to help me get through a period of being understaffed.

Now I think of them as a permanent part of our team. I was pleasantly surprised to see our Sales Associate take so much pride in her work. It feels so good as an Owner to have someone part of your team that wants to win so badly for you, the business and the clients.

Their ability to take feedback is what I think one of the keys is to the success we have with our Sales Associate. She asks for feedback and then executes on it.

They are also so detail oriented so it is so nice to have them come on board and start tracking all our numbers including EFT, leads, conversions, past dues, calls made and total pitches.

We have become super organized since bringing on Gym Reinforcements. Dustin has trained his team on our software to the point that they know it better than me. HA! It s a huge win to be able to rely on someone to do xyz and not have to teach them.

Their follow up is dialed in and it s a blessing to know you will not have to remember who you needed to call or text because they got it done. It s SO amazing!!

One thing I encourage all to do is to give it time. I looked at it as a new employee. Although they come fully trained on our system and lead follow up and converting sales, they need to learn your location's specific process.

So make sure you have a great system dialed in and then teach your Sales Associate how you want that. They will execute. I promise that!

We treat our Sales Associate as one of the team!! We love her!! Dustin and the team knew what we where missing! I am so thankful. Thank you Dustin and Marybeth for having a vision and executing on it.

Life changing for this business owner over here.

Daisy Po oi

Dustin is a WEALTH of information. He's super intelligent, compassionate, and VERY humble. Without his support and guidance, I would be completely lost. He's ALWAYS available whenever I text, call, or email even on short notice. Dustin makes the time and responds immediately when I reach out.

We've employed Gym Reinforcements to manage a huge chunk of our operational needs. Kate is PHENOMENAL and very professional. She handles all of our sales follow-up calls, blasts emails/texts, and helps with lead generation. She has worked very hard to go through our past member list and with our most recent promotions for the month of November, we gained 20+ more members! Thanks to Dustin's GR Marketing webinar, we learned some great tips and strategies for bringing in more sales and we sure did hit it out of the park!

All of Dustin's training webinars are so vital to our growth. Not only to our gym's growth but as gym owners. If you're looking for ongoing professional development, look no further. I trust Dustin 1000% and there's no else that you'd want on your side than someone very experienced, understanding, and knows his $h!T. To be the best, you have to learn from the best. Enough said.

Moe Manavipour and Leila Azimi

We were doing ok with sales and did the typical things any gym owner does. Run Facebook ads for an offer to get leads and do the best we could to convert them to trials.

It was hit and miss as we could not get to them in a timely manner on a consistent basis.
Even when they did a trial, we lost many of them as we could not do consistent follow up to close them.

Our focus was delivering a high-quality product and sales was never our strong suit.
So, my partner and I decided to outsource this part to someone who could be available and consistent and is specifically trained in sales.

We had worked with Dustin in the past and had seen the quality of work he offered in previous training we had done with him.

We figured it can't be any worse than what we had done so far and we wanted to try it for 3 months. It has been over 6 months now and the value we have got is amazing.

Consistent lead follow ups, consistent trial onboarding and follow up to convert to members, and many hours gained out of our schedule to focus on the business.

The peace of mind the team at Gym Reinforcement provides is tremendous value for any gym owner and it will allow them to focus on strategies to take their game to the next level. To set themselves apart in a world with so much competition.

Gym Reinforcements was a great decision for us and the timing was just perfect.

Made in United States
Orlando, FL
25 March 2023